Return items to **any** Swin
time on or before the date
and Audio Books can be re
library or visit ou
www.swindon.go

Ellen Watts

Cosmic Ordering Made Easier

How to get more of what you want - more often

Wilson King Publishers
Banbury, Oxfordshire

Cosmic Ordering Made Easier
How to get more of what you want - more often
Copyright © 2012 Ellen Watts

British Library Cataloguing in Publication Data.
A catalogue record for this book is available from the British Library.

Published in the UK by Wilson King Publishing
ISBN: 978-0956331021

Printed by Print on Demand Ltd, Peterborough
This book is printed on environmentally friendly paper

FSC PEFC

Photograph credits, Lis McDermott Photography
Cover design by Steve Shepherd
Cover Artwork: from a specially commissioned painting entitled 'Cosmic Dreams - The Co-creation of Abundance' by spiritual artist, Anna Watkins

All efforts have been made to observe the legal requirements with regard to the rights of suppliers of photographic and other materials.

Disclaimer

The author of this book does not dispense medical advice or prescribe the use of any technique as a treatment for physical or medical problems without the advice of a physician either directly or indirectly. The intent of the author is only to offer information of a general nature to help you in your quest for emotional and spiritual wellbeing. In the event you use any of the information in this book for yourself, which is your right to do so, the author and the publisher assume no responsibility for your actions or any effect caused by them.

Dedication

I dedicate this book with love and gratitude to
the strange and glorious Universe in which we all live
and which lives in every one of us.

And to you, my precious reader
and the miraculous journey ahead of you.

Preface

I first met Ellen 15 years ago when I was the Development Executive at PHH and engaged her to run our in-house sales, customer service and management courses. She always received super feedback and tangible results and so when I left to become Regional HR and Development Manager at Network Rail and later Head of Training and Development at Threadneedle Investments, naturally I asked Ellen to train for me in those companies also.

By the time I retired from corporate life to start a family we had become good friends having similar professional backgrounds and spiritual interests and we kept in touch. I can verify many of the stories in this book because I have been around to see them happen and witness the results. And then, just a few month's ago, we were the answer to each other's Cosmic Order when events led our paths to come together again when Ellen needed help to type up this book and I needed a positive focus and a new career.

Since then I have listened to and followed Ellen's hints and tips on Cosmic Ordering myself. And I've used the teachings in this book, whilst typing up her scribbles, with some amazing successes like winning a fridge in a national superstore competition and my 5 year old daughter, Katie coming first in a National Bank's colouring competition, to name a couple!

I have brought Katie up to believe in a 'magical' world full of hope and wonder, where her dreams really do come true. And I truly wish, from the bottom of my heart, that she retains this quality throughout her life.

Through this book, Ellen will inspire whole generations to change their mindset in order to get more of what they want more often with her open, honest and real life stories. She is the most positive and fun person I know and her enthusiastic, infectious and uplifting personality is used to best advantage through her coaching and training workshops. She is extremely supportive of people and their goals, a good listener, very caring and she lights up a room wherever she goes.

I am extremely proud to be associated with Ellen and this book. I've always said 'Everyone needs to have an Ellen in their life!' And now, through this book, everyone can! This is going to be HUGE!!!

Sharon Smith

**Owner of Personal Presents and
Cosmic Ordering Made Easier's Virtual Assistant**

Acknowledgements

Writing this list of 'thank yous' has been almost as daunting as writing the whole of 'Cosmic Ordering Made Easier' put together. So many people, so little paper, so many fears of missing someone out, but here goes anyway:-

To **Lisa Cherry**, author of 'Soul Journey' and my book mentor throughout the whole process of getting my experiences and lessons transposed from random scribbles to the printed word and beyond; thank you, thank you, thank you, thank you. There is no doubt in my mind that I would never have finished this project without you.

To **Anna Watkins**, the most talented artist, who is as beautiful on the outside as she is on the inside. Thank you for answering my 'ask' for the perfect artist to design the cover of 'Cosmic Ordering Made Easier'. I have so enjoyed our journey together so far and I am totally thrilled with the amazing creation you have painted for me.

To **Alison Neale**, the Proof Fairy and 'Editor Extraordinaire', whose keen eye and sensible logic made sure that you, my reader, have the very best chance of understanding all my intentions. Thank you for your special gift of speed and accuracy, and for your unwavering enthusiasm for the project.

To **Lis McDermott** of Lis McDermott Photography - Thank you for taking the super shots of me for my profile page. I really hate having my photo taken and wasn't looking forward to our shoot. But your unhurried way and special talent for bringing out the best in women soon had me at ease and I'm delighted with the results.

To **Chris Wilson** of Wilson King Publishing, and everyone involved in transforming my edited manuscript into a tangible book. Thank you for all your support, good humour and professionalism. I recognised long ago that this was going to be a team effort and I applaud you all.

To my wonderful fellow writers of the small and elite group *'I Am a Writer'*, namely **Angelika Breukers, Deborah Lewis-Pummell, Gemma Knott, Isabel Johnstone, Jo Hinton-Malivoire** and **Lisa Cherry** for the waiving of the *'virtual pom-poms'* and for reviewing all the chapters for me.

To **Richard Hovey** of Swindon Coaches, who persuaded me I was *'amazing just as I am'* and perfectly capable of writing a book in a week (in the end it actually took me nearly three) but never the less, I would never have even started without that belief and I thank you for it with all my heart.

To **Lynne Pomeroy,** for constantly, and not *always* so gently, pushing me towards using more of my passion; to **Sali Gray,** herself a writer and poet who, in a more subtle attempt to get me out of the starter's block, bought me the most beautiful purple leather-bound journal with the words *'If you want to be a writer - write'* embossed on the cover; and to **Alison McQuillan** for laying the first stone in the whole *'Getting out of the Cosmic Ordering Closet'* story which culminated in the very book you are holding now (published just eight months after the closet doors opened): thank you all, you are special, special friends.

And to **Sharon Smith** who, when I 'asked' for support for my wrist after handwriting my first 6,000 words, phoned just 30 minutes later and offered to type up all my scribblings into Word. What an amazing gift that turned out to be. Thank you from the bottom of my heart. I can't tell you how much I've enjoyed our working lunches (especially the mushroom risotto) and the occasional all-nighter. And how useful - no, mission critical - your contribution has been.

To **Tracy Longdon,** who provided the missing link for me five years ago when she invited me to lunch only a few days after seeing a Cosmic Ordering seminar in London. I will be forever in your debt for starting me on this path. And to **Victoria Sherston,** my Cosmic big sister, who came into my life 16 years ago to answer an enormous, life changing 'ask' and who has been the answer to my prayers many, many times since. I am always mindful of the enormous gratitude I have that you're a part of my life and for all you've done for me over the years. You are an inspiration.

To all my coachees and workshop delegates, thank you for your willingness to have a go and for your feedback and wonderful Cosmic Ordering stories. You were the proof I needed that anyone and everyone can have the same results as I do, if they follow the same principles and steps. And extra special thanks to **Briony Roberts** and **Sharon Smith** and her daughter **Katie Louise**, for kindly sharing their stories in these pages too.

To all the amazing people who took part, wittingly and unwittingly, in the stories I have told here and those who have influenced me along the way: you are far too many to mention individually, but my gratitude to and for you is none the less for that.

And finally to my husband and best friend **Rich Watts**, whose support, both moral and practical, has allowed me the time and space to bring this book to fruition in such a short space of time. There are no words that can be spoken that could ever express the depth of my gratitude to the Universe for giving me you to share my life with.

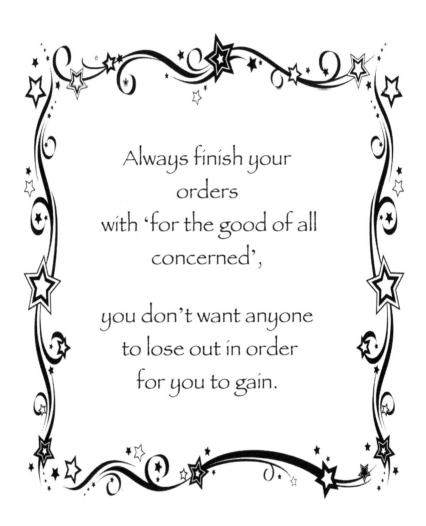

Always finish your
orders
with 'for the good of all
concerned',

you don't want anyone
to lose out in order
for you to gain.

Forward

How to Use this Book

What a pickle I got in when I started writing this book. My head was full of all the amazing stories I wanted to share with you, so you could see for yourself that this *really* works. And more importantly that it could work for you. Then, as a trainer, I wanted to show you how to do it; then as a coach I wanted to hold your hand as you did it for yourself; and then as a mentor I wanted to guide you and help you to learn from my successes - and my mistakes! So I scribbled and scratched, and scribbled and scratched, struggling to get the format just right for you and then ....guess what? I *stopped struggling* and started *'asking'*. I asked the Universe to let me know how I could combine all these teaching styles, how I could be the mentor, the coach, the trainer and the facilitator all in one book. And what you are holding now is the answer.

Part I - The Stories

This section is full of, you guessed it, stories. Real life experiences, mostly my own, but I've also included some stories from people I've coached or trained. I've selected each one carefully for its wealth of lessons. And I believe you will not only find this section hugely motivational, but you will also gain deep insights as you read, because you will be receiving the lessons in the same 'Aha!' way that I received them. And this is immensely valuable.

The stories can be read in order, all the way through, or you can dip in and out of them to gain added insight or belief in any particular area as you perfect your technique. For that reason, I've grouped them according to the main lesson learnt from each story. There's also a 'notes' section after each chapter for you to reflect and jot down your own thoughts, observations, insights and lessons.

Part II - The Workbook

Time for *you* to do some work. In this section, I'm your Cosmic Ordering coach. It's just you and me. I'll teach you the four simple steps to having more of what you want more often. I'll explain how and why things work and I'll guide you through the whole process. I'll ask you questions and I'll expect you to answer them, just like we're in a real coaching session together. I'll help you identify your limiting beliefs and show you how you can prepare, place, recognise and receive your order in spite of them.

This section is not something to *read*; this is something to **do**. Please have a pen in your hand and be ready to really do the exercises to the best of your ability. As you will see, Cosmic Ordering is not a passive activity, but the effort is so, so worth it and so are you. So promise me you'll give yourself the time and do the exercises.

At the end of the workbook you'll find a **'Frequently Asked Questions'** (F.A.Q.) chapter. As I started to coach individuals and deliver my 'Cosmic Ordering Made Easier' workshops, I noticed there were a number of questions that almost always came up at some point during the session. So I figured there was a very high probability that you might want to ask them too during our time together. I've listed the questions in this chapter and answered them as fully as I can. Some answers will be new information and some will simply refer you to a chapter or exercise from earlier in the book with added insights. Either way, I hope you find it useful.

'In a Nutshell' - These pages are intended to be an *aide-mémoire'*. It's the four steps, with the briefest explanation of the most salient points to remember. My hope is that you'll keep it handy and refer to it as a prompt as you hone your skills.

Of course, it may be that you're already an experienced Cosmic Orderer and don't really need the motivation of the stories or the hand-holding step by step guide of the workbook. Or maybe you're a tad impatient and just want the 'how to' in a quick and easy to read format. Or perhaps you have an emergency order to put in that just won't wait until you've read the whole book. Well, if that's the case then please, by all means, read this section first and just refer back to parts 1 and 2 when you need more depth in a particular area.

And finally, the last chapter in the workbook section is called **'Where Do I Go From Here?'** Well, largely that's up to you, but in this section I offer some thoughts, signposts and resources that you might find useful if you wish to continue your journey with this wonderful phenomenon or with your personal development in general.

I do hope you'll find this format helpful and that you and I will become like old friends through these pages and that you'll visit me often. Whether for a technique refresher or a motivational boost, whatever you need, I'll be here for you. To help you to get more of what you want - more often.

And remember, if you order it, it *will* C.O.M.E.

Cosmic

Ordering

Made

Easier

Here's to the journey!!

Shall we begin?

Enlightenment

'According to Vedanta*, there are only two symptoms of enlightenment, just two indications that a transformation is taking place within you towards a higher consciousness.

The first symptom is that you stop worrying. Things don't bother you anymore. You become light hearted and full of joy.

The second symptom is that you encounter more and more meaningful coincidences in your life, more and more synchronicities.
And this accelerates to the point where you actually experience the miraculous.'

Deepak Chopra

---

*Vedanta represents the philosophical portion of the ancient scriptures of India, the Vedas. The basic teaching concerns the ultimate identity of the individual soul with the Supreme Soul. The goal of Vedanta is for the seeker to have the direct experience of his or her true nature, and it is held that each and every one of us is qualified to have that highest illumination if we are willing to put forth sincere and intense effort.

Contents

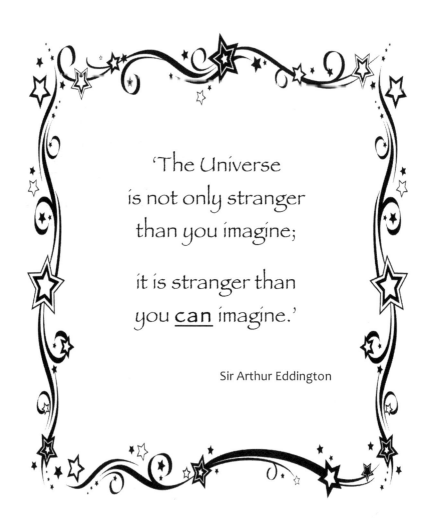

'The Universe
is not only stranger
than you imagine;

it is stranger than
you **can** imagine.'

Sir Arthur Eddington

1

What is Cosmic Ordering?

What is Cosmic Ordering?

Essentially, it's asking the Universe for what you want and it arrives. The term was first used by Barbel Mohr* in her book 'The Cosmic Ordering Service' but the science (or should I call it an art?) has been around forever. In the Bible, it was referred to as miracles. No doubt, at some point, it was regarded as sorcery or witchcraft. Actually, Wayne Dyer had an interesting take on the word 'sorcery' in his book 'The Power of Intention' when he noted that the word literally means 'those who live of the source', which is not a bad way to think of Cosmic Ordering.

And it's since been written about, in some form or another, many more times over. The book 'The Secret' refers to the 'Law of Attraction', which is akin to Cosmic Ordering, while other writers like Wayne Dyer refer to it as 'manifesting'. It's all the same thing really; it's asking the Universe (and when I say Universe, I'm equally happy if you want to substitute that word for Spirit/God/Allah/Source/Cosmos /Angels/Fairies/Higher Self or whatever else works for you) for what you want or need and it will come for you. It's that simple.

Notice I didn't say *'easy'*. If it were *easy*, we'd all be doing it already, without any help from the likes of me. No, it *is* that *simple*, but it isn't *easy*. But then you'll have already noticed that this book is called 'Cosmic Ordering Made *Easier'*, not 'Cosmic Ordering Made Easy'. It's not the Cosmos's fault or the ordering mechanism that makes it tricky for us; it's our own doubts, fears, scepticisms, jealousies and limiting beliefs that get in our way.

It is my sincere hope though, that through this book you *will* find it easier and that once you begin to get the proof your sceptical ego needs, you will experience more and more abundance in your life, whatever that means for you and however you want that to be.

For the Good of All Concerned

One of my own deep-rooted fears that held me back from writing this book for a long time was the thought that someone might use these principles with bad intentions. As far as I can tell, the Universe doesn't care who you are, what job you have or haven't got, how much money you make or how well connected, educated, thin or good looking you are. It doesn't make judgements. It treats every order according to how it's put in. And this means there could be the potential for some unscrupulous people to use it to the detriment of others - and that would not be a good thing.

However, I've come to the conclusion recently that the potential of this knowledge as a force for good in the world far outweighs this small fraction. But to help prevent any adverse results occurring by well-meaning but inexperienced orderers, I want to make this clear right now, right here in this first chapter:- **It is my sincere wish that you finish every order with the phrase 'for the good of all concerned,'** thus ensuring that no one should ever lose out in order for you to gain.

This was always very important to me as I placed my orders, especially ones for money, as I certainly didn't want anyone to die in order to leave it to me. And as you read this book you will see that not only is this perfectly possible from a Universe of limitless abundance, it's also a totally desirable outcome and the only one that brings lasting peace.

The Principle of Giving

Another thing that I would like to mention before we get into the specifics of Cosmic Ordering is the principle of 'giving'. Be generous with your time, your contacts, your attention wherever you can. Really listen to people, be considerate, respectful and kind and notice the little things you can do to help. Why? Well firstly, because it's the right thing to do; secondly, it makes you feel good and to that end it is its own reward; thirdly, you may be someone else's order and finally, you are sowing the seeds that allow the Universe to work its magic. I often call it *'giving back'* but in truth it's more a case of *'giving first'*. Your act may directly come back and benefit you, but more often it has a knock on effect - like the ripples caused by tossing a pebble in a lake they spread and touch far beyond what the eye can see. What you give out will always come back to you - that's part of the Law of Attraction. It may not always come from that person or situation; in fact many times it will not. But it will come.

A Couple of Words of Caution

Something else I want you to be aware of before you start reading the stories is this....you're going to get excited!! OK, you may think, why is that a word of caution? Surely that's a good thing! Well yes - and no. It's great that you will be excited and once you start ordering for yourself and experiencing amazing results you will be more excited still! And naturally, you will want to share your excitement and your successes with everyone and show them how they can do the same. And that's nice but, and here's where the word of warning comes, be careful. Not everyone will be ready to hear about all the wonderful good luck that you are having and some with most definitely *not* be ready to hear that they can do the same, particularly if things are not going so well for them at the moment. I know, they're just the ones who need it the most, but that is how it is. They must come to learn about it in their own time and in their own way. It's not for you to thrust it upon them.

Even people you'd really think should be happy for you, like your family and friends, may be surprisingly jealous and this can express itself in sarcasm and even attacking behaviour. So my advice, while you're building your confidence in your Cosmic Ordering muscles is to only share your orders and successes with like-minded people. Cosmic Ordering can work for anyone and everyone but not everyone will understand and you can't make them - even if you think they really need it.

The other little thing I've found is that generally, people don't care to be referred to as your *'order'*. No doubt many of the best successes you will have will involve a wonderful person coming into your life either to bring the skills, contacts or relationship that you *'asked'* for.

In these cases I've found that unless they are very comfortable around the concept of Cosmic Ordering and sometimes not even then, they visibly prickle if you call them (no matter how gratefully) your 'order'.

I think it's because the natural feel of the word 'order' sounds like a command. Rather like you've summoned them and they had little or no free will but to obey you. This is nonsense of course - they have complete free will. It's just the sound of the word. The same people are usually delighted to be referred to as 'the answer to your prayers'.

And lastly, a final word of caution: You can have *anything* you want, but you can't have *everything* you want. I'm not sure why that's the case, but I do know it to be true. I'm letting you know that now, before we start, to manage your expectations and to avoid any disappointment in the future.

But don't worry; what you *can* have is more than enough, and *everything* you need. You'll soon see what I mean as you walk with me through the following 'Story' chapters, starting with how it all began...

* Bärbel Mohr (5 July 1964 – 29 October 2010) was a German author. She published 20 German books (self-help books, children books, stories) - including the best-selling Bestellungen beim Universum (The Cosmic Ordering Service), translated into 14 languages so far and a German audio edition – which, combined, have more than 1.5 million copies in print. She actually wrote The Cosmic Ordering Service in 1995 for a small group of people and distributed it as a Xerox copy. In 2006, Noel Edmonds (UK TV presenter) would credit her book with turning around his career.

Part I

The Stories

'If you don't know the trees you may be lost in the forest,

But if you don't know the stories you may be lost in life.'

Siberian Elder

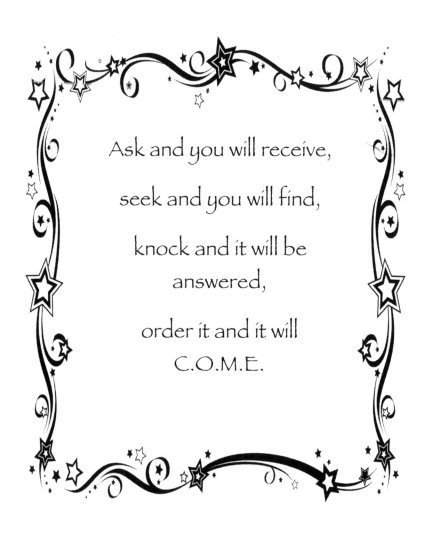

Ask and you will receive,

seek and you will find,

knock and it will be
answered,

order it and it will
C.O.M.E.

2

The Day the Penny Dropped

I've been Cosmic Ordering for as long as I can remember. I didn't call it that back then; in fact, I'm not sure I called it anything. But I was certainly always aware that I had the ability to ask for what I really needed and it would come about. And I have always considered myself a very positive and, above all, resourceful person. In fact, my maiden name was Needs and I always liked the play on the old adage 'Needs is the mother of invention'.

This positive attitude had been instrumental in creating a very nice life where many of the things I saw for myself as a child had materialised: lovely husband, our house in a beautiful village on the edge of the Cotswolds, dogs and horses and my own training company (which came about from the most amazing Cosmic Order that I might tell you about later if there's time).

But it was in 2007, a few months after moving into our new house (another amazing story for another time) that I had lunch with a very good friend, Tracy Longdon. Tracy and I had met a few months earlier at a belly-dancing course at our local college. The course had only been four hours long and there were a dozen or so ladies at it, but Tracy and I had stood next to each other at some point in the day and found very quickly that we had the same sense of humour. We swapped numbers and became friends.

When I got there, I found Tracy excited by a workshop she'd been to a few days earlier about Cosmic Ordering. I'd never heard the term before, so I asked her what it was. She explained:

'It's rather like asking the Cosmos for what you want and the Cosmos delivers it to you - a bit like a big John Lewis in the sky!'

When I look back to that moment, given that I had already had a wealth of evidence that just such a phenomenon existed, my answer was surprisingly sceptical.

'If that really works, where's my million?'

It was a phrase I would hear over and over again from others in later years when I was the one explaining. For now though, Tracy looked at me with all the disdain of someone that had just been on a workshop about the subject, and said,

'It doesn't work like that!'

'OK,' I said, suddenly more curious than sceptical. *'How does it work?'*

'Well,' she said, seeing that she now had a more willing student, *'if you ask for a million, but you don't believe you deserve it, or think that it would change you, or that you would lose your friends, you would effectively block your order from coming!'*

An interesting discussion followed, as did a sumptuous lunch. Tracy really is a wonderful cook.

The next morning I was in the shower and I started to replay in my mind the conversation from the day before. Do you ever do that? I call it 'replaying the tapes'. I hadn't discussed it much with Tracy, but what she had said about limiting beliefs stopping me having a million had bothered me. I didn't understand. I thought I had very positive beliefs about success and money. I've never believed it to be the root of all evil, only the love of it. To me, money was just a tool that could be used to do great things. I had seen poverty and I knew that you can't do much good for others if you're worrying about where you own next meal is coming from. The more I thought about it (still in the shower) the more I puzzled, until I decided: 'Let's be absolutely clear about this - what *exactly* are my core beliefs about money?'

And this is what I listed so proudly to myself:

'I'll always have enough.'

'I'll always get by.'

'As long as I can think and talk for myself, I'll always work.'

'I'll never go under.'

And if we're short one month -

'I'll always pull it out of the bag.'

And as I listed them a sudden moment of piercing clarity dawned on me:

*'I'll always have **enough**!'*

*'I'll always **get by**!'*

*'I'll always **work**!'*

Oh my goodness! These core beliefs that I had lived by, even said proudly out loud to people, that I had believed were *so* positive (and let's face it, they were, compared to most people's) were actually *very* limiting indeed, as in they literally 'put a limit' on how far I was able to go - and it was certainly enough to stop a million coming anywhere near me!

What a revelation!!

So right there (still in the shower), I decided to do an experiment and place an order, just like Tracy had explained to me, for the good of all the people I taught and coached. I felt I owed it to them. After all, I'd been teaching goal setting and positive thinking for years - and this was clearly something that I needed to explore more in order to be of more service to the people who looked to me for the answers.

Right there, I decided to hold those newly identified beliefs out of the way and order in spite of them. And I put an order in for £10,000 to be in my bank account by the end of the month for the good of all concerned.

That was about 7.30am. At 8.00am (I was still blow-drying my hair) the phone rang. I was working from home that day and on any other such day I might have been tempted to let it ring. (*'You can wait till I start at 9.00!'*) But today, newly excited by the prospect that my £10,000 could arrive at any moment, I dashed, wet haired, to the phone.........

'Good morning, ElleRich Training Ltd, how can I help?'

It was my wonderful long time friend, Victoria. (*'Ah, not my order then. Never mind.'*) Now Vic and I go back a very long way. In fact, she's a huge part of another amazing story that I will definitely tell you about later, about how ElleRich Training started. In the ten years we'd been friends, I'd trained for her in every company she'd worked for, but I'd never trained for her in her current company as it had not been their policy to use external trainers.

'Vic!! How are you?'

'I'm great Elle, and so happy because I have it cleared that you can come and do some training for us!'

'Wow that's great, Vic - I'd love to work with you again.'

(Can't be the order though, because even if I could fit in £10,000 worth of work before the end of the month - unlikely - it would be invoiced at the end of the month and paid the end of the following month. No, this can't come from work, but still, it's very good news indeed.)

'What did you have in mind, Vic?'

'I thought a leadership programme. Perhaps spread over the next six months. I've got about twenty team leaders, so perhaps two groups running side by side.'

(Ah, *definitely* not the order - but still a jolly nice piece of work and I feel very grateful).

'Can you come in and see my HR Director? She'd like to meet you and discuss ideas for the programme.'

'No problem, Vic, I can come in tomorrow afternoon.

It's been a great call and I'm excited by the prospect. OK, so it's not the order, but it's still a wonderful start to the day. And then she said it………..

'Oh my goodness, I nearly forgot to say... I've got to get it in this year's budget. I know we don't know exactly how much it's going to work out yet, but Elle, could you invoice me today for, say

£10,000 and I'll get it paid into your bank account before the end of the month.'

My heart stopped. I looked at the clock. Less than one hour after putting my order in, it had arrived. And for the exact amount and timeframe I had asked for.

I said goodbye to Vic and immediately rang Tracy. (I think I got her out of bed - she was certainly sleepy.) I can remember saying to her, *'Look what you've done, look what you've done!'* You see, as happy as I was that my order had come, I was also acutely aware that life would never be quite the same again. I could suddenly see the truth that there were no excuses, no circumstances, no inherited 'genes', no crutches, no blame, no other people standing between me (and by 'me' I mean 'you' too) and anything I wanted to be, do or have. In fact the only thing that had ever stood between me and anything I wanted to be, do or have was my own 'limiting beliefs' and now it turns out that they were bypassable all along. And that fact was exhilarating to me, but more than a little scary. The only thing I kept thinking was *'This is HUGE!'*

I can't remember much of the rest of that day - I'm sure I carried on in the office, doing what had to be done and I'm sure I'll have had a smile on my face - but it was next morning in the shower, when I had the time and space to reflect on the events of the day before, that I suddenly had the thought:

'Hang on – by the time I get taxed I won't actually get £10,000. Blow, I should have asked for £15,000 to get £10,000.'

No sooner had I finished the thought when another voice (me) said:

'Now you're just being greedy!'

The owner of the first voice (me) mentally jumped back and pointed at the owner of the second voice (me) - hope you're following this OK - and said;

'Aha!! Another limiting belief! How interesting - so you think asking for more than you need is "greedy", do you? Amazing!!'

Thrilled with the notion that I had named and shamed another limiting core belief standing between me and abundance, I made a decision there and then (still in the shower) to order another £5,000 for the good of all concerned.

I knew it couldn't come from Vic as she'd said that was her budget spent so I knew this was a completely new order!!

I could hardly wait for the phone to ring.

It didn't!!

And at 12.00 I left to drive to Theale to meet Victoria and her HR Director. It was great to see Vic and we chatted as we walked to the meeting room. *'Don't go without saying goodbye,'* she said. I promised I wouldn't. I paused for a moment before going in – I wanted to tell her about the whole Cosmic Ordering thing but I hadn't been able to yesterday on the phone because I'd been too shocked and now there wasn't time. No, maybe I'd save the whole thing for lunch together - another time.

The meeting with the HR Director went brilliantly and my 12 module Team Leader Journey (TLJ) programme was born.

Afterwards, I found Vic back at her desk and she offered to walk me back to Reception. On the way, she paused several times to introduce me to a member of her team or one of the leaders I'd be training. Vic is so great at inclusion; it's one of the things that makes her such an iconic leader. The last person we detoured to was Mark............ .

> *'Elle, this is Mark, he's my counterpart. He does the same role as me but inbound customer service as opposed to outbound. Mark, this is Ellen, she's coming in to run a series of training days for us for our team leaders covering every aspect of customer-focused leadership.'*

What happened next was truly amazing. Mark stood up and shook my hand but was speaking to Vic as he said:-

> *'Blimey, Vic - my team leaders could really do with that,'*

> *'Well how much have you got left in your training budget?'* Vic replied,

> *'Only £3,000,'* he shrugged.

'Well, I've got £2,000 - so that's £5,000. That'll get you one set,' Vic said and, turning to me, finished with:

'Elle, could you invoice me for £15,000 instead, and we'll get Mark in on this too!!'

———— ❦ ————

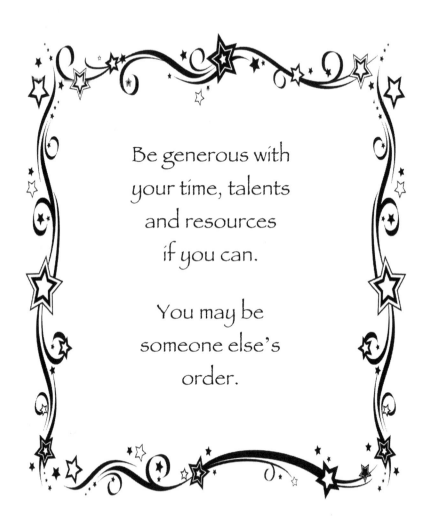

Be generous with
your time, talents
and resources
if you can.

You may be
someone else's
order.

Lessons Learnt

What did you learn from this story chapter? Make a note of your own thoughts, observations, reflections, insights and action points here:-

THE DAY THE PENNY DROPPED

'Those who
don't believe in magic
will never find it.'

Roald Dahl

3

The 'For the Good of All Concerned' Stories

I'm still in awe of those two days. I'm not sure any story will ever again be so gripping, so thrilling and so shocking to me as that of the £10,000 and £5,000 stories, simply because of the revelation of the importance of how you ask and the impact that has on the sheer speed and accuracy of the order.

Yes, I learnt an enormous amount that day. And I have continued to learn (and relearn) ever since. The following two short stories are about something I had to *relearn:* The necessity of saying *'for the good of all concerned'* at the end of each and **every** order. And I want to talk to you about this lesson early in the book simply because it *is* so vital.

In fact, Tracy had explained its importance to me during our lunch together and her explanation was clear: *'You don't want anyone to lose out in order for you to gain,'* she'd said. *'For instance - you wouldn't want anyone to die in order for you to get your money.'*

I agreed, *'I certainly wouldn't!'*

I'd been very careful to add the phrase when I ordered the £10,000 and the £5,000 and I have continued to do so for all the amazing orders I've done since. Only twice have I ever forgotten (to my knowledge) and this is what happened.

The Story of the Hoof Pick

I have two horses. I keep them in a field that I rent, very near to my home. I don't bother bringing them in to their stables to groom them, preferring to take a bucket full of my grooming tools out into the field to give them their 'beauty parlour' while they munch their grass. It's a peaceful time. I start at the top with their manes and tails and then work over their body, using a variety of combs and brushes, mitts and cloths and a little massage here and there as I work my way along their backs and down their legs. The last thing I do is pick out their hooves and then I paint them with a nice coat of hoof moisturiser - beautiful.

Now to pick out their hooves requires a 'hoof pick' (makes sense), which is a piece of metal about the size of a pen with the end bent over to allow it to scrape the mud out of the cavities in a horse's foot and this makes the horse more comfortable.

The problem was, because it was always the last thing I used, with all the grabbing of brushes and cloths by the time I got to that point I could never find the hoof pick. It had invariably slipped down between the brushes to the bottom of the bucket, where it hid quietly defying my poking and shuffling until, in frustration, I would have to tip the whole lot out on the grass to find it.

It was on one such occasion that I held it up after finding it and contemplated its thin and dark appearance and wondered if I was not the only person who had such challenges.

> 'What I could really do with,' I thought, 'is a great big fat-handled hoof pick that wouldn't fall down so easily - in a nice bright colour so I could see it too. Pink would work well.'

I guess in a way I wasn't planning to put it in as an order so much as I was vowing to look out for such a thing or maybe to buy some pink duck tape and 'modify' the one I had, given that I'd never seen anything other than the type I had just described for sale anywhere.

But the next morning Rich and I were walking our two dogs along a beautiful quiet part of the Ridgeway near our home. We had only walked a few yards from the car when I saw something pink lying on the track. No - could it really be...?

> 'My hoof pick!!' I declared as I ran off ahead to pick up a lovely Bentley padded handled hoof pick in a two tone pink.

'How could you possibly have known that was a hoof pick at that distance?' Rich said, catching me up. *'It could have been a sweet wrapper or anything!'*

'Oh, because I ordered it yesterday,' I said excitedly. *'I didn't realise I had, but I did say'* *"What I really need is..."* *now I come to think of it.'*

'Oh,' he said – as if that was perfectly reasonable. *'And just how did a pink hoof pick get out here?'*

'Well someone must have come out for a ride this morning,' (It's always good to carry a hoof pick when you ride out in case your horse picks up a stone in their hoof.) *'and they must have dropped it.'*

And that's when I realised.... That *'someone'* had had to lose their hoof pick in order for me to get it. Because I hadn't really realised I was putting an order in, I hadn't finished it properly with *'for the good of all concerned'* and someone else had paid the price for my omission.

After a swift reprimand, I forgave myself, of course, because:-

a)   A hoof pick only costs around a fiver.

b)   It was a valuable lesson and one I vowed to take good note of from now on.

c)   What's done is done and feeling guilty helps no one.

d)   It's important for the soul to forgive everyone (and that includes yourself).

e)   It's a great story to tell of a spot-on Cosmic Order delivered in less than 24 hours!

f)   It's a *great* hoof pick and I never need to tip out my bucket to look for it any more.

The Story of the Foundation Pencil

Never again though!

Until the next time that is. Hey, don't you judge me too harshly; sometimes we *all* take a few bumped heads before we remember to duck for a low beam in the holiday cottage.

This time I was on the way to a dog show with Rich and our young Rhodesian Ridgeback girl, Sumatra. It was a championship show at a prestigious British showground.

At some point in the journey I pulled down the visor on the passenger side to check my make up in the little visor mirror. It was all in place but I frowned at a big red patch on the side of my nose. It was the last reminder of a spot or bite I'd had and was all but healed, but to me it dominated my face and I was not pleased with my overall look. I contemplated my makeup emergency kit in my handbag: mascara and lipstick - no help at all.

> 'The trouble is,' I rationalised to myself, 'it's impossible to take a bottle of foundation in your handbag as it would just leak or get all messy. Powder's no good because I don't like the flat matt effect; I prefer a more natural outdoorsy look. And concealer sticks are no good for this sort of thing because they 'stick' in the dry scab of the spot and now instead of a red patch you have a concealer pencil coloured patch, all clogged up. Yuk - no thanks!

> 'What I really need,' I speculated, 'is something that would lubricate the dry patch first - something like a balm and then a foundation that would carry safely in my handbag without getting all messy, that would just glide over the area without sticking in it, and in just exactly the right skin colour for me.'

I spent a few more seconds wondering what such a product might look like before snapping the visor back up, resigned to being 'Scarface' for the day.

When we got to the show ground it was heaving with visitors. It was a beautiful sunny day and people from all over the country were filing off with their dogs to the appropriate show tents.

As usual, I headed straight for the Ladies'. It was a posh showground and the loos were a permanent structure and very nice indeed. There were several cubicles, the sinks were arranged in a circle in the middle of the room and there was a long stretch of mirror along one side with a narrow shelf in front. As I went to enter a cubicle I noticed a big fat two-tone eye pencil on the floor near one of the cubicle doors, the sort that has two sharpened ends in two complimentary colours. I nearly picked it up but I thought, *'Do you know what? I haven't ordered an eye pencil. I don't use eye pencils, I prefer shadow. I'll leave it, that's clearly someone else's order.'*

I must admit I was surprised to notice it was still there when I came out of the cubicle with all the other women coming and going. To me, it was odd that no one had picked it up. (Perhaps because it was on a loo floor!)

I decided to be helpful to the person it was intended for so I picked it up and put it on the ledge in front of the mirror. Now if the person who lost it or the person who needed it came in they'd see it, I thought. Then I washed my hands, brushed my hair, despaired at my dry red scabby patch and left. It was a couple of hours later, just before I went in the show ring, that I had the urge to go again......

I went to the same Ladies'. It was even busier than before and this time I queued for a cubicle, after which I washed my hands and went to check my face in the long mirror with the ledge. I was genuinely surprised to notice the eye pencil was still on the ledge just where I left it. I was baffled: *'All these women and no one had picked it up. How curious. Was it such an awful colour?'* I picked it up for a second time but now really looked at it for the first time and laughed out loud.

It wasn't an eye pencil at all but a brand new, still had the plastic on it L'Oreal foundation/concealer pencil with two ends. One end was a rich moisturising barrier balm to coat the 'blemish' (L'Oreal's code word for scabby spot) and the other end was a creamy colour true match foundation.

> *'Well, what do you know? It was my order after all!'*

There are many reflections and lessons to be learned from this small story. Here are a few to get you started:

a) I love that it was **exactly** what I'd asked for, even though I didn't know what I was asking for (but I had been very specific in what I *wanted*) - a most useful lesson for later.

b) I love the fact I missed it the first time - because I didn't recognise it. What a lesson!!

c) I wonder how many orders we all miss because they didn't come packaged in the way we expected.

d) I love that no one else took it – I'm not sure what the lesson is there, I just love that they didn't.

e) Of course, I *didn't* love the realisation that I had accidentally put an order in again without finishing *'for the good of all concerned'*. To be fair I'd never done it in the car before - but that was really no excuse, and that would definitely be the last time.

Lessons Learnt

What did you learn from this story chapter? Make a note of your own thoughts, observations, reflections, insights and action points here:-

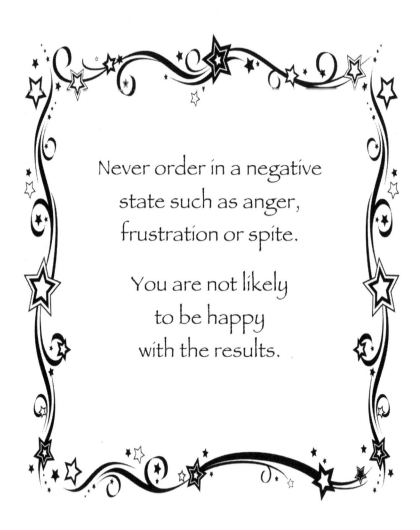

Never order in a negative
state such as anger,
frustration or spite.

You are not likely
to be happy
with the results.

4

The 'Just What I Asked For', but 'Not What I Wanted' Stories

I nearly named this chapter *'Be Specific, Be Very Specific!!'* before changing it to one of my husband Rich's favourite quotes: *It's just what I asked for, but it's not what I wanted.'* He's an IT Programme Manager and he uses this phrase to mimic customers whose ambiguous IT remits have resulted in disappointment when their project delivers exactly what they had requested but it doesn't accurately meet the needs of their business. And it's a lesson I've learnt well over the years too. Training, as I do, in communication skills, I've seen it again and again in sales, customer service and management scenarios. Oh yes, miscommunication is a wonderful thing.

When it comes to Cosmic Ordering the rule is clear: *be careful what you wish for.* In fact, these three short stories should carry a Government Health Warning:

Not being specific could seriously damage your order!!

The 'Two Trees Down' Story

One sunny but windy spring day, not very long after the £10,000 and £5,000 incident, I was standing at the bottom of our garden with a large mug of black coffee cupped in my hands. We'd moved into the bungalow during the winter so this was our first spring here. It was a beautifully mature garden - and by mature, I mean it was full of enormous trees and shrubs (and weeds). So I often started my work-at-home days in the garden with a morning coffee, just strolling around, planning and dreaming what we might do when we could afford it.

That particular morning my planning attention was concentrated on one particular area near the bottom of the garden. It was home to a small forest of conifers (about a dozen) of various heights, all crammed into an area no bigger than our living room. No doubt when they were first planted they weren't expected to grow so tall but now their foot-wide trunks were so close together I wondered how they could all survive. *'Their root systems must be so stunted,'* I thought.

In fact, I found myself contemplating the amount of sway on two of the tallest (40+ ft) giants as the wind rocked them back and forth. I was reminded of the Twin Towers, which I had once read could sway three feet in any direction in a gale. I decided the trees really needed to come down. If the wind ever caused them to fall they could do an enormous amount of damage, whichever direction they went. The fence line, a dry stone wall, the potting shed, the summer house and the hot tub house were all within a 40ft radius of their bases. At that moment we couldn't afford to have a tree surgeon in to do it, so I decided to put an order in to have the trees down, but I didn't want to pay anything for it, for the good of all concerned.

Of course, what I *meant* was for someone to come in with a big chain saw and take the trees down professionally - but I must admit I wasn't completely disappointed when the next day both of the 40 footers had fallen over in the biggest overnight storm. Miraculously, they had both fallen diagonally and in the only space possible where they could do no damage - right between two buildings. They'd missed every single structure. It wasn't quite what I meant, but I was secretly pretty thrilled with the results. And Rich enjoyed chopping them into logs and all our neighbours with wood burners benefited too.

The 'Big Plants' Story

So that story had a happy ending but some of my other 'not specific' orders have not been quite so fortuitous. A few weeks after the crashing trees incident, I was back in the same spot with another mug of morning coffee, reliving the amazingness of the likelihood of the trees' fallen paths and also contemplating the vast empty space their disappearance had left behind - a space that needed filling before the weeds did it for me.

Since we moved in we'd been so very blessed by our neighbours, all keen and very able gardeners, who'd given us so many seedlings and tiny cuttings. But this was a big space and I felt something bigger was needed here. 'What I really need,' I decided, 'is someone to give me some really big plants - and I don't want to pay anything for them, for the good of all concerned.' And I started my walk back to the house.

As I walked through the conservatory doors my office phone was ringing. It was Rich; he was working onsite at some offices in town.

'What are you doing?' he said.

'I'm just about to start work.'

'Can you come in to where I'm working - in the Shogun?' he asked.

'I could. Why?'

'I've got something for you,' he said.

'Oooh what?' I asked excitedly. But in my head I thought: 'Big plants, big plants, big plants!!'

'You'll see,' he said.

So I went. And when I got there, I found Rich co-ordinating an office shut down. Boxes of files and IT equipment were being shipped out and I adjusted my guess to some useful equipment for our training company that was going spare that was destined for pick up. 'Here you go,' he said, and he pointed towards two huge and very uncared-for rubber plants in pots. 'No one wants them,' he explained, 'so they're going to get thrown in the skip. I thought they'd go alright in our conservatory.' I felt my nostrils flare slightly. Covered in dust and with about ten yellowing leaves hanging limply on each plant, the skip was possibly exactly where they belonged, but I respected Rich's generosity of spirit in trying to 'rescue' them and together we negotiated getting them safely in the 4x4, losing as few leaves as possible as we posted their spindly extremities through the sunroof.

As I drove home at 20 miles an hour to cut down on the vibrational impact on the few remaining leaves, I laughed out loud to myself (and the Universe) as I shook my head and said: 'Outdoor plants, I meant - really big outdoor plants!!!'

The 'Two Cars off the Drive by Christmas' Story

Fast forward to three weeks before Christmas the following year for my next lesson in remembering to include all the detail. I was leaving for work one morning and I cast my eye, as I did most mornings of late, over the four cars crammed on our front drive and garden.

No, we hadn't come into money; this eyesore was the result of a couple of strings of events. The Shogun was Richard's, the little green Mazda was mine. The deep metallic red Nissan Skyline had been imported from Japan (Rich's little business on the side) but the buyer had fallen through and now, thanks to the economic downturn, it wasn't selling. And we had bought the burgundy Cavalier for £2,000 when the Shogun needed to go in for about three weeks to have some repairs because we had to wait for the parts to be shipped in from Japan. A hire car would have cost a lot for three weeks so we had the 'smart' idea of buying a cheap car and then selling it again once we got our own car back - costing us next to nothing. Good plan, except that the Shogun had been back six weeks now and still the Cavalier was on the drive. No one was buying cars, it seemed.

With three weeks to Christmas, funds low and, even more importantly, nowhere for our Christmas guests to park when they came to visit I was suddenly sick and tired of our front garden looking like a garage forecourt and so, in frustration, I hastily put the order in as I got in the car:

'What I really want is two of those cars gone off this drive before Christmas.' What was I thinking? It could have gone down any number of ways, but it went down this way.............

I was driving to Gloucester that day and it was cold, I remember. As I drove down the long A419 towards Birdlip, I noticed the heater gauge going up and up. 'That can't be good!' I opened the window; the engine sounded OK but the smell was not pleasant. 'Still, we're moving OK - so keep going,' was my thought. I was the trainer and I could do without breaking down and having the AA out roadside. I didn't want to be late.

As I drove various dashboard lights came on and bleeping things bleeped. But the engine was still running so I kept going. I tried to keep it steady: *'If I can just get there then I'll call the AA who can sort it out for me while I'm training.'* It was a good plan and it was working until I got to the Birdlip roundabout where I was forced to stop and that was all too much for my lovely Mazda and it was all over. I coasted to the hard shoulder and rang the AA.

The AA man was a very, very nice man and after a brief roadside discussion he agreed to tow me to where I was training so I could be on time and he would attempt to fix it in the car park for me.

Sadly though, he couldn't. Apparently, because I'd continued to drive it so long after the problem occurred, I had effectively *'fried'* the engine. It was beyond economical repair. Result - exit one green Mazda from our drive.

Oh well, in some ways it was good that we had the Cavalier as a 'spare' car. I could have that for now. It wasn't ideal as we were hoping to sell it to replace funds in our account, but at least we didn't have to pay out for a new car for me. It was the best positive spin I could manage. After all, it could have been worse.

And then it <u>was</u> worse..........

Just two days later I was training in Bristol. It was very cold and halfway along the M5 the temperature needle started getting higher. *'Oh no!! Surely it can't be happening again? Well, I'm not going to make the same mistake twice!!'* I pulled straight over onto the hard shoulder to call the AA. *'This time I will have caught it in time and saved the car!!'* But as I turn the engine off and the smoke bellowed from under the bonnet I was not so confident and sure enough I'd blown a gasket and it was, you guessed it, beyond economical repair!! And that was two cars off the drive in three days.

Of course I'd meant for the Skyline and the Cavalier to be gone and I wanted to sell them for a decent price, but that's not what I'd asked for. I'd asked for two cars off the drive by Christmas and that's exactly what I'd got. It was a very expensive (but ultimately priceless) lesson.

P.S. The positive upside of this story was I was allowed to drive the Skyline for a while until it finally sold to an enthusiast a few months later. Wow - what a great car!!!

Lessons Learnt

What did you learn from this story chapter? Make a note of your own thoughts, observations, reflections, insights and action points here:-

Spot your
limiting beliefs and
order in spite of them.

And if you have a really
stubborn one,
order like crazy until
it explodes for good!

5

The 'Something for Nothing' Stories

The 'Furnishing the House' Story

In terms of time frame, this story happened very shortly after the £10,000 and £5,000 revelation. Still fascinated by the realisation that only our limiting beliefs stand between where we are and where we could be, I went on the rampage, seeking out my limiting beliefs as if they were the enemy, because that's *exactly* how I saw them.

The next major one I identified turned out to be a biggie with roots like a seven year old ragwort plant (you pull it up one year and it leaves 50 little root tips ready to form brand new plants next year). It reminded me of Earl Nightingale and a recording he made in the 1950s called 'The Strangest Secret' where he says that the mind is like fertile soil. He goes on to explain that it returns what we plant in wonderful abundance: if we plant crops, we get crops; if we plant weeds, we get weeds. Success or failure, a concrete, worthwhile goal or confusion, misunderstanding, fear and anxiety: the soil (mind) doesn't *care* what we plant; it just *returns* what we plant.

So I found this deep rooted spreading weed in my soil (mind) called 'You don't get anything for nothing,' common name 'There's no such thing as a free lunch.' And I'd created all sorts of subspecies around it like 'Always paying my way', 'You get what you pay for' and so on and so on. So I started a Cosmic Ordering campaign against this very personal enemy and for the next three years almost everything I ordered finished with the words 'and I don't want to pay anything for it, for the good of all concerned.'

My aim was to bust the limiting belief for good as I knew this was necessary for my growth and to understand what at another level I already knew to be true. That is, that *the Universe is limitless, it doesn't need money, it creates*, and most importantly from my standpoint, *no one need lose out for you to have. There's more than enough for everyone.*

I didn't start lightly either. We'd just moved into our new bungalow; we'd remortgaged and stretched ourselves to the limit to get the place we wanted, which was amazing. But we moved in December 2006 and in January 2007 Northern Rock had fallen over and suddenly the world was a different place as the nasty seed of the mind-weed called 'recession' was planted in the minds of the masses.

Plus, caught up in the joys of moving, I'd taken my eye off the business ball and now the two events combined were reflecting in our bank account (and not in a good way). And to cap it all, we'd just heard that the bonus that Rich normally received each year in June from his work had been frozen. No one would receive a bonus that year.

So money was short and, at the same time, I needed things for the new house - lots of things. And so I made a list:

- A doormat
- A hand mixer
- A George Foreman grill
- A breadbin
- Tea, coffee and sugar canisters (ours had got broken in the move)
- A 6 seater wooden patio table and chairs
- A gas barbeque
- A garden strimmer
- A slow cooker
- A petrol lawnmower
- New bedding
- A sack truck

- A book case

- A front room rug

There were so many things that needed to be specific that I suddenly decided that the easiest thing to do was to get a catalogue and choose from there as if I was going to reserve and collect them in store.

And sure enough I found everything I wanted in the Argos catalogue. So I chose and put big circles around everything and then pulled out the pages and put them in a folder. When I was done, I put an order in for everything I'd circled in the Argos catalogue, finishing with *'and I don't want to pay anything for them, for the good of all concerned.'* One big order and it totalled nearly £1,500.

What happened next was more bizarre than I could have ever imagined. I had expected the things to come in dribs and drabs. I supposed they would be 'like' the items I had chosen. I certainly didn't expect all of them to be new (and I would have been more than happy with that). I was not prepared for that evening, when Rich came home from work and said:

'Guess what?'

'What?'

'My boss called me today and said how unfair he thought it was that I wasn't going to get a bonus this year, seeing as my project is one of the only ones that's made the company money...'

My ears pricked up; maybe Rich was going to get a bonus after all.

He continued: *'He said he couldn't give me a bonus because it was a company-wide ban and totally out of his hands...'*

My heart sank again.

'So what he's done is he's nominated me for some internal customer service award instead to recognise my contribution!'

'Great! Can we eat it?!' I said ungraciously.

He laughed. *'No, but I think I'll get some gift vouchers with it or something.'*

'Oh well,' I thought. *'Perhaps £25 or maybe even £50 will come in handy - but hardly exciting.'*

'How much? And who for?' I said.

'I don't know,' he said. *'I'll find out tomorrow when the email comes through to say if I got it.'*

He got it.

And it was £1,500 of Argos vouchers! We took the pages from the folder to Argos that Saturday, filled in the codes and came home with the whole lot. And how did I feel? Well, have you ever heard the expression *'It was like all my Christmases had come at once'?* Yes? Well it was a lot like that - only tenfold!!!

The 'Riding Holiday' Story

Do you ever write New Year's resolutions? For years I would write a whole list that would look remarkably similar each year:

- Lose three stone
- Save more money
- Exercise more
- Take more 'me' time
- Get on top of the garden
- Ride Meg (my pony) more
- Finish decorating the hall or kitchen or bedroom etc.
- Get more business
- Read more books

OK, sometimes it would be more specific. After all, I was good at setting goals - but it was invariably a list about what I'd like to do and have and get done and the fact that most years the list looked pretty similar might give you the clue that most things didn't happen.

So this year things were going to be different. As we approached the last few months of the year, I reflected on the amazing couple of years that had just passed and I started to look forward to the one ahead. I decided to write a list of a different sort. Rather than a list of resolutions it was a list of Cosmic Orders and read as follows:

What I really want is:

- A two week top quality, luxurious, fun and active adventure or safari type holiday that we'd both enjoy in South Africa, New Zealand or Australia and I don't want to pay anything for it.

- The person, resource, event to really motivate me to lose three stone.

- The person, resource, event to motivate and give me the confidence to ride my pony again.

- Rich to take more of an interest in riding so that when Narna passes on we can get one for him to ride and we can ride out round the village together.

Even though it was only December, when I finished my list I put my order in for the year finishing it with *and I don't want to pay anything for them for the good of all concerned.* And then I put the list in a folder on my bookshelf with thoughts of ticking things off throughout the year as they came in.

A few days later, I'd already marked in my calendar that our local Countrywide store was holding an equestrian event on Tuesday (my work-from-home day). What that meant was there was 10% off all horse feed that day and there would be suppliers there giving advice and free samples. They held such an event a couple of times a year and I liked to go if I could.

Now, as it happened, on this particular day I was very busy. I couldn't really spare the time, but I really wanted to go. After all, 10% is 10% when you have two large dogs and two horses to feed. So, late in the day, I made the commitment and drove the ten minutes to the store with strict instructions to myself that I had ten minutes in store and no more.

I loaded my trolley with my horse and dog feed and ignored the temptation to schmooze with the suppliers and chat with the lovely staff I know so well. But just as I was about to join the queue at the checkout, I noticed a stand in the centre of the store - a prize draw!!

Now I'd often entered the store prize draw before on days like this and in the past I'd won a bag of dog feed and a horse rug and other similar value prizes - and I do like winning things. So I took a step towards it, quickly scanning the banner for when it was going to be drawn. My heart sank as I noted that, unusually, it was a national competition, to be drawn at the end of the month after all the stores had had their equestrian days.

> 'Rats!' I thought. 'What are the chances of winning a national draw? C'mon, you haven't got time for that - you're in a hurry.'

But immediately I answered myself.

> 'No chance at all if you don't enter it!' How true!

So I quickly filled in the postcard with my name, address, email and how many horses I had, and popped it in the small slot in the huge drum. I didn't even stop to read what the prizes were - after all, any prize is a good prize in a free draw.

This was the email I received on Friday 11th December 2009 at 16:59

> 'Hello,
>
> My name is Pip. I am writing to inform you that you have WON the equestrian event prize draw and therefore have won:
>
> An In The Saddle Holiday at Horizon for two in South Africa worth £4,500.
>
> Please could you make contact with me between 8.30am - 5pm, Monday - Friday to discuss claiming your prize.
>
> I do hope this email finds you well and excited.
>
> Kind regards...'

Wow!! All my orders answered in one fowl swoop. We chose to take the holiday in September 2010 to coincide with our 22nd wedding anniversary and to give us both plenty of time to lose weight and get fit.

It was an amazing holiday in every way and we didn't pay for anything.

- I lost three stone easily, because I wanted to be as light and as fit as possible to be able to get the most from the holiday and be kind to the horses.

- We had riding lessons so that Rich could ride on the holiday too (he'd never been on a horse before) and that gave me the confidence to start riding my own pony again.

- He was so good at it, and he enjoyed the holiday so much, that *he* suggested that when Narna moved on to the big pony paddock in the sky, the next horse we got should be one big enough for him to ride. (Result!!)

So guess what? I don't bother with New Year's Resolutions any more - just New Year's Orders.

Oh, and the 'free lunch' issue? Well I can wholeheartedly now confirm that they do exist. I have had over 100 free lunches *'for the good of all concerned'* since I identified that particular negative belief, including one a week before our African holiday when I went to the gym (Rich and I had joined to get into shape for the holiday) and there was my name printed up on the board.

'What's this?' I said to the member of gym staff on Reception. *'Why's my name on here?'*

'Oh,' she said, *'Dave (a trainer at the gym) has nominated you for Member of the Month for doing so well with your weight loss and fitness goals.'*

'Really?' I said excitedly. *'Fab!!'* Then I added, 'Is it just fame and glory?!!'

'Oh no,' she said, *'you win a prize too - this month it's a free meal in the hotel carvery!'*

I just couldn't help grinning.

And so we booked to have our glorious *free* three course lunch together, in the hotel carvery, right before driving off to the airport for our *free* two week riding safari holiday in South Africa.

Oh, how I've loved busting this particular limiting belief!

Lessons Learnt

What did you learn from this story chapter? Make a note of your own thoughts, observations, reflections, insights and action points here:-

_____

_____

_____

_____

_____

_____

_____

_____

_____

_____

_____

_____

_____

_____

_____

_____

_____

_____

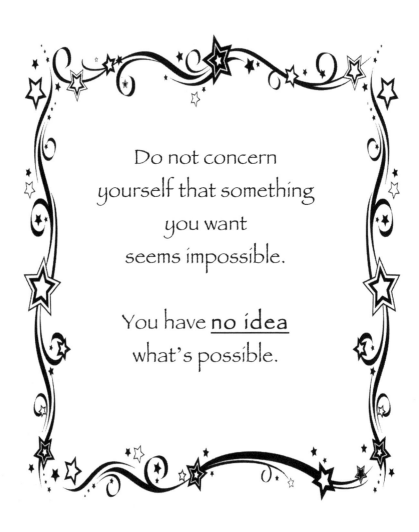

Do not concern
yourself that something
you want
seems impossible.

You have **no idea**
what's possible.

6

The 'Nothing is Impossible' Stories

Since I've started coaching others to order for themselves, one of my favourite things is to see people place an order for something that they believe is 'impossible' and then see it arrive.

I think that's because I know what a tricky one it is. The word 'impossible' seems so definite, doesn't it? So final, and yet I've had the proof time and time again that the Universe doesn't acknowledge 'impossible' and that we have no idea what can happen if we would only remove that limiting belief (because that's all it is) from our path.

The problem is we are often programmed to do exactly the opposite. We support 'impossible' with our repetitive self talk of *'how hard it is to...'* or *'such a thing doesn't exist'....* and so on.

The Story of the Perfect Pony Paddock

One such time for me personally was shortly after I moved into our new home. I wanted to move my horses much closer to us to save me time and petrol so I began to look for a suitable yard or field.

At first, I was very optimistic. There were many fields around the village and I was confident one would be available to rent. I really wasn't expecting it to be hard. I started making enquiries, but it turned out trickier than I expected. Hardly any of the fields were owned by the people living in the houses adjacent to them, and even tracking down the owners was proving challenging.

A determined soul by nature, I made postcards with an appealing picture of my two horses on it and an appeal for information about fields or yards and posted them through the letterboxes of everyone in the village with the message **'Can you help?'** Surely someone, somewhere must know something. *'I only want a field, for goodness' sake! Any field would do!'*

I had one positive response from my card drop and although it was still a mile away from the house and not ideal, I moved the girls there as at least it was nearer than where they'd been. But it was low ground and flooded easily and that, coupled with many other undesirable factors, meant I was less than happy there. Turns out 'any field' *wouldn't* do after all - good lesson.

So I continued to look, desperately in fact, but everywhere was either full or inappropriate. And, in the end, things came to an uncomfortable impasse at the field I was at and I felt strongly motivated to remove myself swiftly.

I relocated my girls to a friend's yard temporarily while I continued to look in my own village, so now I had to travel twice the mileage I had before I moved them in the first place, and it was winter-time. It was all very frustrating.

I found myself saying to people who asked:

> *'It's so hard. I can't believe it - all this land around us and nothing's available!'*

> *'I never dreamt it would be this difficult, why is this difficult?'*

> *'It's impossible!'*

> *'It's not for want of trying (followed by the long list of activities I'd done to find somewhere).'*

> *'It's all so frustrating!'*

And then one day I listened to myself as I was talking to a friend about it on the phone (playing the now well-grooved record called *'It's impossible to find a field in Blunsdon!'* with all its verses) and I realised what my self talk about the whole situation had become - and it wasn't pretty! Plus I realised for the first time that I had never even put a proper Cosmic Order in for it; I'd never even defined exactly what I wanted. I reflected on how this could have happened and came to the conclusion that in the beginning, I probably didn't even feel I needed to. After all, I had been confident it would be *easy*, a piece of cake, to find a field in a village surrounded by fields.

I was confident that my own resourcefulness and ability would unearth the perfect plot and that it would all just fall into place. But slowly, as life had unfolded with indifference, my mindset had been gradually eroded by the rejection and difficulties until it had become downright toxic and all my beliefs about the situation had become ones of difficulty and impossibilities.

I had been struggling with this '*I can't find a field*' problem and I was complaining about it, worrying about it, trying to solve it but every response I received just confirmed my belief about it being so hard. In other words, I got to be right. Oh, how us human beings like to be right.

I was suddenly reminded of a Zig Ziglar story that I'd heard on a cassette tape of a live seminar he did in the 90s. (I think it was called Goal Setting.) In it, he explains how to Cook a Frog. If you throw a frog into boiling water he would jump out, right? Of course. But if you put him in a pan of tepid water, he'll stay. Frogs like water and he'll stay where he's comfortable. Then, if you gradually turn up the heat, warmer and warmer, the frog becomes dreamier and dreamier until by the time it's uncomfortable for him, it's too late. He squats to jump out but he literally gets cooked in the squat.

And that's what happens to us too - and I'd let it happen to me. Suddenly I saw the whole thing differently and, like the frog that suddenly finds enough consciousness to kick his legs and jump free of the pan, I realised I needed to stop struggling and start asking.

To start with, I listed for the first time exactly what I needed this paddock to be:

1. A short walking distance from the house. (No more car journeys with muddy boots.)

2. On high ground with good drainage. (No more flooded fields.)

3. Easy, clean, fresh water supply. (No more carrying buckets for miles.)

4. Just a grass field of two or three acres with two field shelters or stables, no other people, no other horses in the same paddock. (Although other horses in adjacent fields would be nice.)

5. No roads in between the stables and field. (No more crossing roads with a horse in each hand.)

6. Not too remote or scary to be in on my own. Perhaps adjacent to houses with lovely people who will keep an eye out for the girls and enjoy them being there.

7. Safe boundaries with no way that people could get in and horses get out, and a gate that opened onto an easy riding path, not a road.

8. And to cost no more than £100 per month, for the good of all concerned.

Once the list was written, I looked over the map of the village to see which ones met the criteria. There was only one that fitted the bill - it was at the top of the hill, with new fencing up and two stables on it. Perfect. There was only one snag - it was already full. I had made enquiries over six months earlier, before I'd moved to the low level flood plains and I'd given the girl I'd spoken to there my number, but everyone there looked set to stay.

For a moment, I was thrown. What to do? Compromise on what I wanted or put the order in for something that I 'knew' was impossible? Which would you have done?

I decided to put the order in for what I *really* wanted and leave the rest to the Universe. And that evening I had a call from Mandy....

It turned out that Mandy rented the very field I was interested in, plus the others adjacent to it, from various different land owners. In turn she sublet the individual paddocks to other people and it had been one of these other people (Roma) I'd seen and given my number to six months earlier.

Mandy was calling to say that a month ago Roma had decided to move her horses to somewhere with a ménage (a training area where she could work her horses). Apparently, Roma had given Mandy my number but Mandy had 'lost' it - but had *just a few minutes ago*' found it again and she was ringing to see if I was still interested in a paddock. (Interested? That was an understatement!)

As I walked over to meet her that evening, I wondered which two paddocks she would offer me out of the eight or so possibilities. Any would have done as they all met a lot of the criteria I'd listed. But to be absolutely perfect and in line with my order, it needed to be the two directly behind the bottom of the bungalows at the end of our little crescent. That way the three neighbours at the bottom of the crescent could keep an eye on the horses and it would be the shortest walk from home. Well it turned out they were the very two she had free and, even better, when I told the neighbours I'd be moving the girls in, one lovely couple offered to let me walk through their garden each day, meaning the paddocks were now less than 50 yards from our house, and another neighbour offered to fill up my water buckets every day with his hosepipe - and what a blessing that is. And in return Meg and Narna keep the crescent's gardens fertile with regular barrows of pony poo, so everyone's happy.

Especially me. What a very valuable lesson that one was.

It was a lesson that came back to me the first time I coached Briony Roberts. Briony is the M.D. of Blue Bear Marketing in Lechlade, Gloucestershire. We'd met at the very first Athena networking meeting I went to and she asked me to do a single Cosmic Ordering coaching session for her. She'd considered herself very positive and that she had a good idea about how to place a Cosmic Order but felt that a really important 'ask' was eluding her and she felt stuck. This is her story:

Briony's Story

'I met Ellen for my first coaching session on how to master the art of Cosmic Ordering on a Tuesday lunchtime in May 2012. I'd heard her deliver a talk about it at an Athena Business Lunch meeting and was absolutely bowled over by her personal anecdotes. They were truly incredible and I found her infectious enthusiasm, coupled with a down to earth approach, very reassuring.

During our session, I shared my already prepared list of Cosmic Orders with Ellen and at the very top of the list was the one that I wanted the most. It was really, really important to me and I had wanted it for some time. The only problem was, I believed it to be impossible.

I was running my PR business from home and had done so for some time, but I'd really had enough of working on my own. I wanted - no, needed - the stimulus of other people around me and the validation of being a 'proper business' that I felt having an office would bring.

The problem was, I'd been searching for such a shared office space for ages and I knew there was nowhere available in Lechlade (where I live). In fact I was certain that there were no offices on the rental market within a 10 mile radius - certainly none that I could afford, anyway.

I was fairly surprised that Ellen paid little attention to my explanations of why it was impossible and instead got me to focus on exactly where I would like my office to be if I could afford it and if one were available. After some resistance, I listed my preferences and I put an order in that day for *'a shared office in Lechlade with lovely friendly people where I would feel comfortable and validated and I didn't want to pay anything for it, for the good of all concerned.'*

The next evening at 'Read, Red & Rosé', a local book club gathering, I mentioned how frustrated I felt working on my own all day to Julie (whom I thought was a stay-at-home mum and housewife) and she said: *'Would you like a desk in our new offices, just down the road? We've been saying we could really do with the place looking busier, but we're not allowed to sub-let rooms due to a clause in the lease, so we can't charge you any rent. But it would be lovely to have you around - you'd be doing us a favour!'*

And it was as simple as that. My first major Cosmic Order was fulfilled within 24 hours and I haven't looked back since.'

Briony Roberts
Director of Blue Bear Communications

Lessons Learnt

What did you learn from this story chapter? Make a note of your own thoughts, observations, reflections, insights and action points here:-

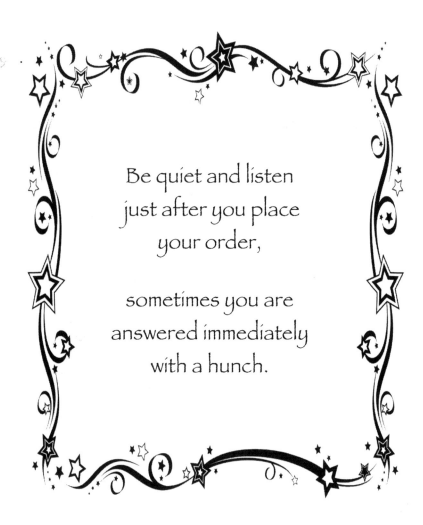

Be quiet and listen
just after you place
your order,

sometimes you are
answered immediately
with a hunch.

7

The 'Follow Your Hunches' Stories

I've really been looking forward to writing this chapter as it vocalises an important concept that I truly believe in, and that is that the Universe is not something *'up there'* or *'out there'*, it is something that is *'everywhere'*. And that means that we are *a part of it, not apart from it*. We are in it and it is in us.

What this means in practice is that we will very often be or know our own answer. I have long given up the notion that I am 'clever' or 'talented' or 'special' when I come out with little gems of wisdom when I'm coaching or writing. I've learnt that my very 'best ones' come through me. Sometimes it almost feels like cheating, like an inner voice is telling me what to write and what to do.

'Aha!' moments, flashes of inspiration, hunches, gut feelings - call them what you will. But my advice to you is to listen to them. Why? Because they know stuff, and the times when I have spontaneously followed my hunches, straight after putting an order in, have brought about some truly spectacular results.

Here's a special story that I think makes the point very well. Enjoy!

How ElleRich Training Ltd. Began

This story happened long before I was aware of the term 'Cosmic Ordering'. In fact, I was unaware of a great deal of the things I am certain about now. But looking back on the incident, I can see I did enough things right for the most spectacular and synchronistic colliding of events to occur. (In my mind now, I picture it like two tectonic plates colliding and pushing up to create a new and immensely beautiful mountain range). Curious? OK, here's the story.

It was 1996 and I was working at British Gas Service. I'd started there as a Customer Service Adviser as Rich and I were running our own Multi Levelling Marketing business in our spare time and my retail management career was just too demanding hour wise and too poorly paid.

This role in a 300 strong contact centre was the first time I'd ever worked 9-5 with weekends off and it took some getting used to. But the biggest benefit to me was that the work stayed at work and when 5.00pm came, I had no obligations or worries to take home with me and that was a huge bonus.

The job itself though was mundane, but I carried it out with my usual enthusiasm and it wasn't long before I caught the eye of Pete, my supervisor. One day he approached me and asked if I'd be interested in being a Customer Service Trainer. Apparently they were looking to pull a training team from the business for a ten month project. *'Absolutely I would!!!'*

There's a ton of stories I'd love to tell you about how the next ten months as a British Gas trainer unfolded, but for now suffice to say I *loved* it!!! And it gave me the wonderful opportunity to become computer literate in things like PowerPoint and email and files and disks, which had never crossed my path before in the retail world.

In the end, there were twelve trainers selected from the business and we trained in pairs. As we neared the final weeks, gradually each pair returned to the business until only my partner (Martin) and I were left training. But eventually even we had to return to our desks. The training was over.

It was a desk that seemed smaller now. And a role that seemed smaller and more restrictive too. As trainers we'd swanned around, not beholden to set breaks or even a team leader. We'd walked around like freelancers, set our own agendas and co-ordinated and liaised across the ranks. To go back to the predictable routine and tight regime of my previous role was suddenly unacceptable.

And so it was one morning that I found myself at my desk looking around and thinking: *'It's time to move on - but what?'* My C.V. was looking more than a little messy: a career in retail management, sales and sales management, recruitment and now contact centre work. I decided to list all the jobs I'd done and then run two columns alongside: 1) what I loved about it and 2) what I hated and why I'd eventually left.

What became apparent was I loved the customer service, the sales, the people development, the training, the coaching, the networking, the co-ordinating and liaising and what I hated was the paperwork and the politics. *'What can I do that gets me all of column 1, but none of column 2?'* I asked, almost out loud.

And instantly the answer came back, followed by an incredible urge to leave *'right now'*.

I looked at the clock; it was *almost* lunch time. So I gathered up my things, signed off my computer and left. I walked right out, not knowing where I was going really, but I walked with a purpose to my little royal blue £500 Mini (which always sounded like it had a tool box loose in the boot when I went over speed bumps at the top of town - there was no tool box!!!)

I got in and drove three miles to town (over said speed bumps), parked up and walked down Commercial Road (a long, straight road in the town centre, lined with banks, estate agents and recruitment consultants). I walked at speed; my face looked determined. I would have looked to anyone like a woman on a mission. And I was; it's just that I wasn't *entirely* sure what that mission was at that point.

I stopped outside Pertemps and looked for a while at the ads in the window. *'Have I come here for a new job?'* I was puzzled.

I went in. The lady at the reception desk was familiar to me as she often came into British Gas. British Gas used Pertemps all the time for all their temporary staff. My mouth opened and I started talking and found myself hearing for the first time, exactly what this brand new plan was going to be ...

'Hello, I've just decided I'm going to become a freelance customer service and sales trainer. So I thought I'd pop in and let you know, so that if you ever get a phone call from a client saying their trainer has gone sick for the day, I can step in and save the day for them.'

Even as I said it I remember thinking: *'That doesn't sound like much of a plan! I can't think that would happen very often.'* However, my thoughts and her answer were interrupted by a voice from the back of the office.

The voice was saying excitedly, *'Stop! Stop! Don't let that lady go! I've got something here!! Came in this morning! Hang on - don't let her go!!!!'*

In shock, both of us swung round to see a frenetic permanent consultant called Renée scouring and shuffling her paper-covered desk with the look of a woman possessed.

'Here ... here,' she said, holding up a small white job card which she proceeded to read from. *'Wanted: Freelance Customer Service and Sales Trainer - £300 a day.'* Looking up, she said: *'It just came in this morning!!!'*

I reacted in the only way I could think appropriate - I laughed. *'Very funny,'* I said. I believed she was being sarcastic, pulling my leg for coming in with such a ridiculous idea. The rest of the conversation went like this:

'No, really, it came in this morning!!'

'Yeah right - I used to be a permanent consultant - you don't get things in like that.'

'Not normally, no!' she agreed, *'but it did. Have you got your C.V.?'*

'No, I haven't got my C.V.,' I said, suddenly believing she might be telling the truth. *'I didn't even know I was coming!!'*

'Well go home and get one.'

'I can't, I'm at lunch; I have to go back to work.'

'Well pop one under the door this evening and I'll get it to the client tomorrow.'

And that was how I left it. I drove back to work, finished the day with my secret held so tight I thought I would burst and that evening I created my freelance trainer C.V. profile with my very limited IT skills and popped it under Pertemps' door at about 11.00pm that evening.

I can't remember exactly when Renée called to tell me the client wanted to see me, but it wasn't very long, and I went to meet Victoria Sherston, then the Operations Director of an outsource contact centre called Phonebox UK. We got on like a house on fire and halfway through the interview I decided to tell Vic how events had unfolded, to which she smiled and said: *'Want to hear another funny thing? I don't even use that agency. We use another one in Commercial Road to fill our contact centre seats but Renée from Pertemps has been calling me and trying to get a foot in the door with us. Up to today I've turned her away, but the morning you went in she'd rung again and this time I decided to give her a chance.'*

It turned out that Vic had been a freelance customer service and sales trainer for a number of years herself, but now with three children she had decided to go back to corporate life for more stability and had entered into a new business (Phonebox) as the Operations Director. She'd planned to continue working with her existing training clients by moving them over to Phonebox and had expected to deliver the training herself under Phonebox's banner. But the operations role had proved demanding and she'd decided to find a freelance trainer to take on work for them on an adhoc basis.

That morning she had used the opportunity as a test for Renée, explaining that she wasn't going to pay Pertemps for it because it wasn't a permanent role but that if Renée was successful Vic would offer Pertemps some contact centre seats to fill.

I'd never thought of this next bit before today. The conversation between Vic and Renée had taken place approximately one hour before I put my order in to *'get me out of here'* (although my listing of past job likes and dislikes had started earlier). I always thought that I was the instigator of this order, but in writing the story down for the first time, it could have been Victoria, needing the position filled or even Renée, desperate to fill it to get some more business from Vic. Who knows? Maybe all of us played our part and like a great big cosmic matchmaking service, the Universe paired us all up for the good of all concerned. Who knows exactly how that all worked? I do know that the results were monumental. Vic and I are still friends and I very much doubt I'd be sitting here and writing this for you now if it hadn't happened.

I drove back to British Gas after my interview and handed in my notice. And the following week, on 1st April 1996, ElleRich Training Ltd. was founded.

Lessons Learnt

What did you learn from this story chapter? Make a note of your own thoughts, observations, reflections, insights and action points here:-

The Universe helps
those who help
themselves.

8

The 'Follow the Lead' Stories

The next six months directly after I left British Gas and set up my own training company went very well indeed. I had some training days from Victoria and it had given me the confidence to stand alone as a freelance trainer. Now it was time to step things up a gear and I put a Cosmic Order in for a project. What I *really* wanted, I decided, was something just like I'd had at British Gas. What I meant by that was about a ten month project delivering customer service training to about 300 people. What I got was even more spot on.

The Calortex Contract Story

Later that same day I was driving home and I heard a recruitment advert on the radio for a company called Calortex. The company was made up of Calor Gas and Texaco and had been formed to take on British Gas in the planned deregulation of the Gas Industry in 1998. The radio commercial was advertising a recruitment evening. Apparently the Slough-based company were moving to Swindon and looking to recruit 300+ staff at an open evening at a local hotel. I smiled as I just knew the hotel would be full of British Gas staff looking to jump ship. *'It'll be like a reunion, perhaps I should go,'* I thought, *'and maybe they could do with a hand to train those 300 staff.'*

So I went and it was just as I thought, jam packed with lovely British Gas staff all looking for pastures new. I enjoyed myself enormously, socialising and catching up on the BG gossip, but a few enquiries also led to me putting out my hand to a very handsome man who was the Customer Services Manager of the new company.

I explained that I'd not long finished training most of the people in the room at British Gas Service and asked if he would like some help with the setting up and training of the new contact centre. Looking back, it was a brave thing to do. After all, I'd only been one small cog in a large wheel at British Gas; one trainer of twelve delivering a prewritten programme. Here, I was offering to undertake the whole project, start to finish, under my own company banner.

But it paid off. Not only did I become the sole training provider for Calortex but that contract catapulted ElleRich's growth in so many ways and in so many directions It would take another book to tell you about them all. Some of the journey was very challenging and there were many times I was outside my comfort zone and many more times I thought I'd bitten off more than I could chew. But the growth I went through was all necessary for me to become who I am now and what I do today. And it all started from hearing that radio advert and sticking out my hand to a Customer Services Manager.

There have been many stories since where the Universe has answered my 'asks' with a lead. A name mentioned, a phone number given, a competition to enter, a website, book or venue recommended. I like these types a lot. I see leads as 'clues' that lead to the prize. They're not the answer themselves, but they lead to the answer and all I have to do is go and collect it.

Here's another story to show you the different forms a 'lead' can take and how important it can be to take action straight away. P.S. This one almost went wrong.

The Topsoil Story

One day I was working in the garden on a terraced area, building a dry stone retaining wall, and I noted that, as the wall I was building was higher than what had been there before, I was going to need some topsoil to raise the flower bed behind. It was a considerable amount and to buy it in bags from a garden centre would have cost a small fortune. So I Googled the possibility of buying a truckload and having it delivered. Ouch - still surprisingly expensive considering it was just dirt! Suddenly, I had the 'aha' to Cosmic Order it so I started to plan my order. First, I needed to be specific: how much did I actually need?

I calculated twenty barrows full and, if it was to be Cosmically Ordered, I might as well ask for it to be Blunsdon topsoil. That way I'd know my plants would be bound to grow in it. And I wanted it to be delivered; I didn't want to have to wheelbarrow it from someone else's house in the village. And I wanted it to be sifted and weed free and, as I was in my 'something for nothing' period, I naturally concluded with *'and I don't want to pay anything for it for the good of all concerned'.*

And then I suddenly realised I needed it by Friday so I could fill the bed by Saturday morning, ready to go down to the annual Blunsdon Village Gardening Club's plant sale at the Village Hall. (I always like to support that and get nearly all my plants there for the year.) So the final order that I put in was:

> *'What I really need is twenty barrows' worth of sifted, weed free, Blunsdon topsoil delivered right here on my front drive by Friday and I don't want to pay anything for it, for the good of all concerned.'*

And here's what happened next...

The next morning (Thursday) I started work in my office, which is at the front of my house, and before long I heard what sounded like a tractor outside. *'What is that noise?'* I thought, and I looked out of my window into the street but could see nothing. *'Where is it?'* I was certain this had something to do with my order so I popped out into the front garden to investigate further. Suddenly I could see it was a mini mechanical digger and it was right next door! Now, my neighbour's front garden is long and behind a high fence so it hadn't been possible for me to have seen it from the house. The digger was removing all of their front lawn. (I found out later that they had decided to turn it all over to shingle to allow more room for parking cars.) The result was that accumulating behind the digger was a *huge* pile of topsoil. OK, so it was, at the moment, full of turfs as well, but still, it was lovely looking soil and it certainly couldn't have been more local!

Now the only slight challenge was I wasn't particularly attractive at that moment as I was in my jim-jam bottoms and tee-shirt and hadn't had my shower yet. (I often put in a couple of hours' work before getting spruced up for the day.) I nipped back with the intention of scrubbing up and then popping round to flutter my eyelashes at the gardener to seal the deal.

Imagine my surprise - no, horror - an hour and a half later when I sauntered out to begin my negotiations to see no digger, no gardener and no great big pile of topsoil. It was gone - all gone!! I rushed to the fence - nothing!! All was as flat as a pancake and no one to be seen. *'Oh this was wrong, very wrong!!'*

At that point another neighbour who lived opposite came out and I pointed wildly at the flat soil, shouting, *'Did you see a digger here about an hour ago and a big pile of turfs?'* 'Oh yes,' he said to my incredulous face. *'Wow, what a worker. He's dug all that up, cleared it all into a skip and it was all taken away within the hour - very impressive!!!'*

No!! I was shell shocked. Taken away? But that was *my* order, *my* topsoil. It wasn't supposed to be taken away!!

I was close to being mortified and at the back of my mind I knew it was *my* fault. I'd let my ego (worrying about how I looked) get in the way of accepting my order. Still, what a lesson. Yes, as lessons go it was a corker. *When the Universe presents, take action. Claim your order or it might just go away again.* The Universe doesn't care what you look like anyway. We're all beautiful and perfect just as we are. It was just my limiting belief that had got in the way - now identified as *'I'm not good enough to go outside without my mascara and lipstick on.'* I decided to accept the gift of a super lesson graciously and let go of the disappointment and self blame for messing up my order. The lesson, after all, would go on to serve many others in this book.

However, the next morning as Rich and I returned from our very early morning walk with the dogs, there was the gardener again. He was in next door's front garden, this time with a truck load of shingle ready to lay the drive.

'Aha! A chance to demonstrate a lesson learnt.' Although there was now no topsoil to be had, I felt the urge to overcome my stupidity of the day before. Sending dogs and husband inside, I sauntered over in my scruffy dog-walking clothes and pre-showered hair and face and said,

'*Good morning. I just wanted to compliment you on your work yesterday. One minute I looked out and you were digging, the next minute all was cleared away as if you were never here. Very impressive!*' I smiled.

'*Thank you,*' he said and then, probably interpreting my advance as 'nosy neighbour syndrome', he continued with an explanation of what my neighbours were having done.

I listened, and answered with: '*I must admit I was a bit gutted when I saw all that lovely top soil had gone - I was going to ask you if I could have some.*'

'*Oh no,*' he said. '*What a shame - I had to pay someone to take that all away yesterday - you would have been doing me a favour.*'

'*Oh well,*' I said. '*Some things just weren't meant to be.*'

But in my heart I was gutted all over again. It would have been the perfect order - '*for the good of all concerned*'. My ego had cost him too. '*Never mind,*' I said to him and then I came in and headed off for the shower, still licking my wounds and contemplating my lessons learnt.

I'd hardly got wet when the door bell went. '*It's the gardener with my topsoil!*' I thought excitedly and then answered myself: '*How could it possibly be? Face it - the topsoil's gone. It's more likely to be the postman!!*'

I strained to hear the voices as Rich answered the door but they were incomprehensible. I could hardly towel myself dry quick enough to get out of the bathroom and find out who it was.

'*Who was that at the door?*' I said, trying to sound nonchalant.

'*You are so lucky,*' said my husband. '*It was the neighbour's gardener. Apparently he kept back about twenty barrows' worth of the best soil yesterday, sifted it and removed all the grass and roots, because Pat told him she wanted a flower border around the outside of the drive. But it seems she's just changed her mind and now she wants him to gravel right up to the edge and put big tubs of shrubs round the edge instead.*'

My heart skipped a beat.

> So he wanted to know if you'd like the twenty barrows and If so, could he wheel it round now and put it on our drive to get it out of his way so he can get on with laying the gravel.'

My eyes widened with anticipation. He smiled, '*I said you'd be delighted.'*

And I was!

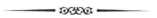

Lessons Learnt

What did you learn from this story chapter? Make a note of your own thoughts, observations, reflections, insights and action points here:-

_____

_____

_____

_____

_____

_____

_____

_____

_____

_____

_____

_____

_____

_____

_____

_____

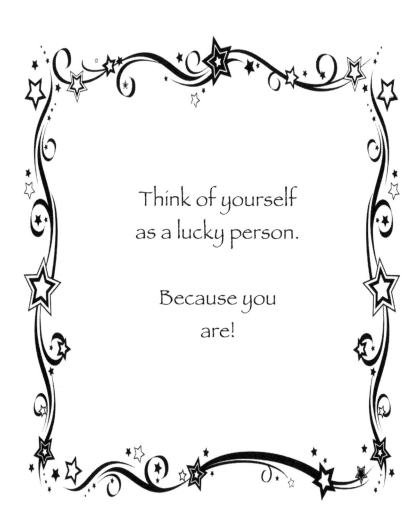

Think of yourself
as a lucky person.

Because you
are!

9

The 'In Your Lap' Stories

I've left this story chapter to last, because in so many ways it's my favourite. Ask the Universe for something very specific and within hours it turns up - a bit like a pizza delivery. The most difficult part is you sometimes have to get up and answer the door and say 'yes please' (and sometimes you don't even have to do that!)

Because of that quality many (but not all) of these orders are small and materialistic and because of that the hardest thing about writing this chapter was choosing which of the so, so many stories and examples I could pick. So here we go with a small selection I've chosen for you. Each, I hope, has a different lesson and all, I hope, bring the exciting realisation and motivation that this stuff really works.

The Ladder and the £10 Note

This is one of the oldest stories in this book. It dates back to just a few weeks after we got married and as it was our 25th wedding anniversary last Wednesday (19th September 2012) I can say it's about 24 years and 11 months old to be precise.

After we married we moved into our first house, a 1930s two up, two down, end-of-terrace in Swindon, Wiltshire. It was an ex-council house and we loved it. But one of the little quirks it had was the external doors. The front door didn't automatically lock, you had to remember to turn around and lock it when you left the house and each evening when we went to bed we would turn the key and leave it in the lock.

The back door, however, behaved like I thought a front door should. If it was shut, it was completely locked to the outside world - unless you remembered to put it on the latch.

So one Tuesday morning (I was an Assistant Manager for Mothercare at the time and worked Saturdays so I had one day off in the week instead) I got up and, still in my dressing gown, I started the household chores. The night before I'd put a wash in the hand-me-down twin tub we'd been given and now had a pile of damp clothes ready to hang out. With morning coffee in hand, I strolled out into the garden to assess the weather for its drying potential.

After a few minutes I detected the lightest of drizzles and turned to come back in, thinking *'Not a good drying morning,'* and then I realised the back door had shut behind me and with the same breath I realised I had not unlocked the front door yet and that the only key to it was in the lock already - but on the inside!

And I was in my dressing gown and it was drizzling.

OK, not one to be taken over by panic, I surveyed the outside of the house for possibilities of a break in. There was one small window open - the bedroom at the back of the house. It was only the small top window, but I was slimmer then and I felt if I could get to it, I could get through it.

Ah, getting to it, that was the challenge. Confident in my resourcefulness, I went and knocked at a neighbour's house. No answer - and suddenly I was aware it was only 7.30am in the morning. *'Too early to be disturbing neighbours,'* I thought, remembering that most were pensioners. *'OK, what next?'* I hadn't got time to hang around until a respectable time and it was drizzling so I thought: *'The shops!'*

Through the tiny alleyway at the bottom of the close was a parade of shops - about a dozen in all, including a DIY/hardware store. Confident in my persuasion skills, I decided to go and explain my plight to the shop keeper who would have a whole selection of ladders and I'd buy one. I'd just have to convince him to let me take the ladder first and then I'd return with the cash *after* I'd broken in. This was a great plan, after all, who wouldn't believe a girl in her dressing gown and slippers?

So I padded and shuffled in my slippers over to the parade of shops, mentally rehearsing my plea as I walked.

Once at the hardware store, I pressed my face against the window. *'Ah yes - lots of ladders. Excellent!'* I tried the door - it didn't budge. For a moment I was puzzled and then the penny started dropping: The closed door, no lights on inside and no sign of staff. The small fact that it was still only 7.45am had temporarily escaped me again. The rest of the world hadn't got going yet. I looked at the opening times on the door - a 9.30am start for this establishment. I rested my forehead on the cold glass of the door. *'What I really need is a ladder - right now!'*

'Are you OK?' A voice came from behind and I swung round to see a cheerful looking older guy in overalls and suddenly I was very aware that I was in a public place in a fairly short dressing gown and slippers.

'I'm locked out,' I explained. *'I need a ladder but the shop's shut!'*

'I've got a ladder on my van,' he said. *'It's through the alley.'* He pointed to a dark alley between two shops that led to the main road. (Now you've got to understand there was a large part of me that heard that as *'Come and see my puppies, little girl, they're back at my place.'*)

But I smiled and followed him down the alley (at an out-of-arms-reach distance) and was relieved to see a council van with a huge ladder on top at the end. *'Hop in - I'll drive you round,'* he said. (Oh, that just breaks all the rules - getting in a strange man's car in your dressing gown! But what are the chances that an unsavoury character with a ladder on his van would just happen to be buying a newspaper when I needed him?) I decided to take the risk.

The next part of the story was nothing short of a comedy sketch. My knight in shining armour was more than a little well padded and so it was clear he would *not* be the one going up the ladder and getting through the small open window. So he did the next most chivalrous thing he could, and he held the ladder for me.

Now I want to put your minds at rest here - yes, I was wearing knickers. However, the dressing gown was short and I had to trust my Sir Galahad's discretion not to peek skyward as I ascended, as ladylike as possible, to the cat flap of a window ... where I encountered my next challenge...

The ladder ended at the window sill and after a couple of attempts of trying to get my leg up to the tiny opening, I realised my only practical option was to go in head first and crawl through until my centre of gravity tipped, whereon I would fall, head first, into the unpacked cardboard boxes stacked high on the other side. It was a good enough plan and it would have worked too if it hadn't been for one small thing (very small - about an inch long, in fact). The metal spike that sticks up in the centre of the window frame and is used for holding the window open caught on the cord of my dressing gown at the pivotal moment and I found myself hanging by it. Suspended in time and over the boxes, and unable to move either way, I had no choice but to forego all ideas of modesty and shout for help.

Once released, I crashed purposefully and elegantly and without harm. How much I exposed I will never know, but I suspect I probably made his day!

Composure regained, I rushed down and opened the front door with the key that was nestled in the lock from the night before (a habit which was immediately changed from that day on) and I went out to assure my knight in orange council armour that I was unhurt and to give him a £10 note for his troubles.

It was a slight wrench to give him the money, as I had exactly £90 cash in the house that I had been saving to buy the material I needed to make curtains for the front and back of the living room. I'd seen the material, worked out the amounts and had the exact money in an envelope ready to go. I was planning to go to town and buy it that morning and that was one of the reasons I was keen not to wait around for neighbours to wake up or for hardware stores to open.

He didn't want to take it at first, but I managed to persuade him that I would have had to have paid more than that for a ladder and that he really had done me the most wonderful favour and when he finally accepted, I could see he was chuffed.

And so was I.

I was back in my home and I'd done the right thing with the money. I felt resourceful, connected, resilient and independent. The only sad thing was I was now £10 short for the curtains. And this was a substantial blow as we didn't have any curtains at all. (At that time we had sheets held up with wooden clothes pegs - a look that came into fashion a few years later, I noted.) There was little point catching the bus to town now I couldn't afford the curtain material. I looked out of the window; it was raining quite heavily.

Suddenly I thought, *'Stuff it! I'll go anyway and I'll take the £80 and who knows, perhaps it will be on sale or there'll be another material I'll like even better that'll work out £10 cheaper.'*

And so I dressed and left for town. It was still raining - which was just as well, or I wouldn't have had my head down as I crossed Queen's Drive to get to the bus stop and I wouldn't have seen the £10 note lying open, flat and wet on the road as I nearly stepped on it. The £10 note that I blotted and blew dry, as I tried to hold in the sheer joy and excitement all the way to Swindon on the bus, before tucking it safely in the envelope with my £80 to buy our curtain material.

I tell you, you just can't make this stuff up!!

The Wrist Support Story

And to finish this chapter I'm going to bring you bang up to date. My Cosmic Ordering coachees love to hear my stories. They like to hear my successes (as I hope you have) because it gives them examples of what they might ask for, lessons of how to refine their own techniques and, let's face it, just a sheer belief boost that it does happen and can happen for everyone.

Even so, can you believe that there are still some times when I don't think to order for myself? And I had such a moment a few days into writing this book. It came about that I made a decision to give myself less than thirty days to write this book start to finish (I do hope you didn't just say *'And it shows!'*)

Anyway, that was quite a challenge, but I knew it was how it had to be.

But even though I booked a whole week out from my business to get started, I didn't write anything for the first two days. I just got sidetracked by emails and Twitter and LinkedIn and phone calls and to do lists. This was not working!!

Then I read a blog about writers who go to a venue each day to write. So on day three I went to our local village hotel with an A4 legal pad and pen and I wrote two chapters by hand. Devoid of the ability to delete, copy and paste, change the font, fiddle with the layout etc. I was left with the art of writing. *Just* writing. And I can write almost as fast as I can talk (and boy, I can talk fast) and so I found, from that moment on, most of this book just wrote itself. My faithful right hand became a secretary that captured all of my thoughts as I spoke them. There was only one problem... I don't know about you, but I haven't written much since I was at school. And by the end of day two and chapter 4, I was in pain. I could write, but to type was agony. How was I ever going to type up the words I'd written?

I mentioned this small challenge in a Facebook post to the lovely support group that had formed as a result of a writer's workshop I'd attended a couple of weeks earlier. My message was of pride and good news about the 6000+ words I'd written. I wanted an 'Atta girl' from the group, but I mentioned the aching wrist too - to which one of the lovely ladies replied (quite rightly), *'Why don't you order something for your wrist?'*

What an excellent point. Why not indeed?

I reflected for a few moments on my personal need for 'struggle' to feel achievement - *'no pain, no gain'* programming - and general thoughts around martyrdom and then I got over myself and put an order in for *'help and support for my wrist so I could have the book typed up for the good of all concerned.'*

I must admit what I imagined would come would be something in the line of a device to either wrap around or rest my wrist on, to help and support it while it carried on doing what I needed it to do. But what the Universe had in mind was much, much better...

About half an hour later a friend called. I'd been trying to get hold of her for a few weeks as I knew she'd been going through the aftermath of a rough break-up. I'd left her a number of messages.

It was lovely to hear from her and I was relieved to hear the only reason she hadn't been in touch was because she'd been away on an impromptu holiday to Haven Doniford Bay with her young daughter Katie.

After telling me all her news and developments she asked after me and the book and I told her about the 6000+ words done in two days but also mentioned the wrist. I'd hardly finished the sentence before she said,

'Why don't you let me type it up for you?'

'Really? I didn't even know you could type,' I said.

'Oh yes,' she said. *'I've got RSAs and everything!'*

('As opposed to RSI's like me,' I thought.) *'No, I couldn't ask you to do that - it's an awful lot of work.'*

'Please let me,' she said. *'You'd be doing me a favour as I'm going to be at a loss this weekend as Katie's going off to her dad's. It will be so hard after having her all week; it would help me to have the distraction.'*

Oh my goodness!! And what a total blessing that has turned out to be! In four short weeks Sharon has turned out to be the answer to more than a few orders of mine to do with this book and I'd like to finish these stories with one from Sharon herself from her Haven holiday with Katie.

The Story of Katie, Bingo and Anxious the Elephant by Sharon Smith

I have always been a 'glass half full' type of girl, but events, combined with life, started to give me negative thoughts and beliefs. Ellen is a very close friend and she had been sharing hints, tips and her successes of Cosmic Ordering with me and I decided to give a 'little' one a go to 'test the water'. What did I have to lose?

Well....... I took my five year old daughter, Katie, to a well known holiday park in the summer holidays and as soon as she saw the 'larger than life' characters, she instantly wanted a small soft toy version. Like every mum on a tight budget, I managed to 'buy some time' and I promised I would buy her a soft toy elephant at the *end* of the holiday if I could afford it.

This was an ideal opportunity, so I put in an order. *'What I really want is for Katie to have an Anxious Elephant soft toy by the end of this holiday and I don't want to pay anything for it, for the good of all concerned,'* I said and, as instructed, I promptly forgot all about it and carried on with our fantastic holiday.

On the second to last day of our holiday, Katie and I were playing 'Rock and Roll Bingo' (a new play on the classic version!) where songs are played and you have to work out who's singing, what song it is and mark it off your card. Well this, coupled with it being Katie's first time playing bingo, was hilarious! I was marking off my own card and trying to keep an eye on what Katie was up to, but I wasn't sure if she was just 'dabbing' off songs on her bingo card for the fun of it!!!

Halfway through the game (with all of this going on and still keeping my eye on both cards) I thought it would be nice if Katie could win her first ever game of bingo and have something really special to remember from her holiday and feel proud of herself.

I put in a very rushed but clear order. *'What I really want is for Katie to win this game of rock and roll bingo for the good of all concerned.'*

Well, the rest was history......... and I didn't have too long to wait. The strains of *'My, My, My Delilah'* started to play and, looking down, I could see that she had Tom Jones on her card. I nudged her and pointed for her to mark it off, which she did. This left only one square (Irene Cara) to give her a full house. This song was from my era so I knew what I was listening for and was willing it to come out!

A few more songs were played and, looking round the hall, I noticed that it was full of people: around 300, mainly adults.

I had everything crossed, which made it difficult to mark off my own bingo card! Suddenly *'Fame, I Want to Live Forever'* started playing and I found myself grabbing Katie's hand, waving it furiously in the air and telling her to shout *'House!'* which she did. I really don't think she knew what was happening, but was whisked along with the activity.

We were asked to go up to the front of the hall and suddenly I had the realisation that we were now standing in front of 300 people and the Bluecoats were checking Katie's bingo card. Had she really marked the songs off correctly? Oops!

Well, after what seemed like an eternity, Katie's card was judged correct (well done her!) Luke, the Bluecoat 'hi-fived' her and she was whisked up on the stage on her own and I was the 'doting mum' smiling back at her. The Bluecoat asked her:

'What's your name?'

'Katie,' she replied confidently. (I was gushing at this stage, and so proud!)

'How old are you, Katie?'

'Five,' she replied.

'And where do you come from?'

'Freshbrook,' she answered and everyone shouted 'Yay!!!' This made me smile as she was so innocent and said the area name instead of the town, Swindon.

The Bluecoat then said 'Well done, Katie. Would you like to choose your prize?' In all of the commotion, I didn't even know what the prizes were. They walked over to the prize 'wall' on the stage and there on the bottom shelf was a big Anxious Elephant soft toy, exactly the same one that she had wanted at the start of the holiday. Katie's face lit up and was a picture. She asked if she could have the soft toy, pointed at it and the Bluecoat handed it to her.

I took a photo of her on stage holding the bingo card and the toy and she was beaming from ear to ear. She was so proud of herself, and rightly so! We haven't heard the last of it since - she keeps on reminding us that she won bingo and Anxious the Elephant has pride of place on her bed every night. The photo is proudly displayed on her pin-board in her bedroom.

I don't think Katie will ever forget that first game of bingo that made her holiday extra special and it will give her lovely memories to look back on for several years to come.

———— ⬦⬦⬦ ————

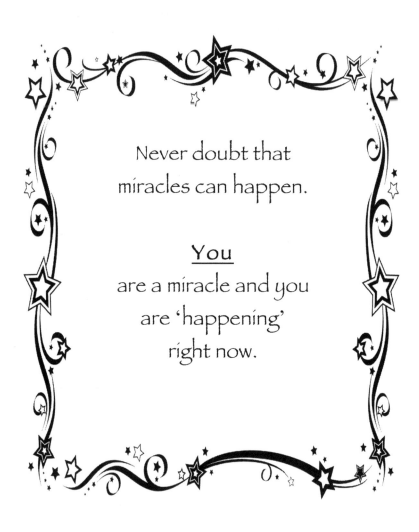

Never doubt that
miracles can happen.

<u>You</u>
are a miracle and you
are 'happening'
right now.

Lessons Learnt

What did you learn from this story chapter? Make a note of your own thoughts, observations, reflections, insights and action points here:-

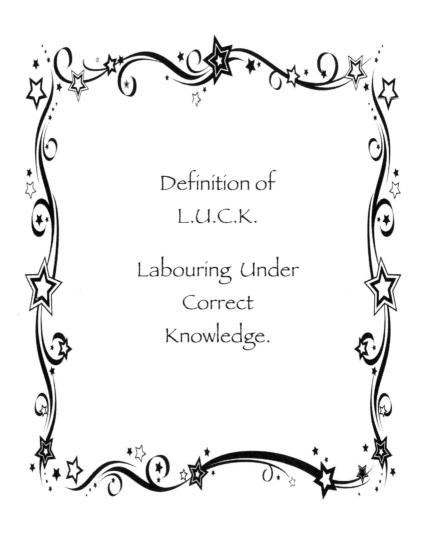

Definition of
L.U.C.K.

Labouring Under
Correct
Knowledge.

Part II

The Workbook

'The secret of getting ahead is getting started.

The secret of getting started is breaking your complex

overwhelming tasks into small manageable tasks,

and then starting on the first one.'

Mark Twain

Only concern
yourself with 'what',
and
let the Universe
work out 'how'.

10

How to Prepare Your Order

OK then, it's time to get on with placing some orders of your own. There are some things I've found that have been very useful to me when it comes to asking the Universe for help and one of the key lessons I've learnt is that it can pay to do a little preparation.

Know what you want

That may sound blindingly obvious, but it's remarkable how many people (myself included, on occasions) have fallen right here, at this first hurdle. And there are a number of levels this *'not knowing'* can occur on.

For some it's a kind of blindness or denial that they want anything at all. Since I have started working with people in a Cosmic Ordering capacity, it has been interesting to note that a number of clients struggle to even write a decent wish list, or when they do it's either full of big stereotypical 'borrowed' goals like *'a million pounds'* or a *'new house or car'* or it's things for family members or partners. They literally don't know what *they* want.

So what do <u>you</u> want?

After all, if the purpose of this book is to help you get *'more of what you want - more often'*, it stands to reason you will need to know what you want.

If this is clearly a challenge for you then my suggestion is to start small to build up your 'desire' muscles with a wish list of a dozen or so things that you would really like right now. What they are is entirely up to you, but I recommend having some small materialistic things on there as well as more intangible things such as health or relationship things. Not that the Universe isn't more than capable of delivering all of these lovely things to you; it's just that tangible things can be easier to define and easier to recognise when they arrive. Plus the thrill and belief levels of such 'quick wins' will help enormously with your more complex 'asks' later.

Exercise: My Wish List

I want you to take a bit of time for yourself to do this now but it doesn't have to be that long - 30 minutes is fine. This is not a week's retreat examining your whole life as you know it (unless you want to) - this is a 'shopping list' you're writing for a visit to the big department store in the sky; treat it with that level of importance. What do you need? What do you want? What do you fancy? And here's a nice one: what do you really need or want to make you happy right now? Write it down.

As you write your list, I want you to be mindful of any thoughts you have as you write and make a note of anything you thought or felt that sounded like resistance. Especially if you felt the urge to modify or take something off the list (or not write it at all). Don't worry about these thoughts; just notice them and write them down and we'll deal with them later.

My Wish List

HOW TO PREPARE YOUR ORDER

I really hope you just took the time to do that activity and you're not just reading on, thinking *'I'll read it all now and then I'll come back and do the exercises later.'* Don't do that. It's only 30 minutes, 15 if you write fast. You're worth more than that. Go back and do it now.

Have you done it? Good. Well done!! Pass, my friend and continue on your journey.

Now we need to choose one thing on your list to prepare for order. Don't worry; you won't always need to go through this whole process. Once you're more practised you will be able to do this on the move as the situation demands (You will still be doing all of the steps, but they will be fast and instinctual) but for now, it's important to understand the steps and why they're there, so that you'll always be happy with your results.

Keep it Positive

Often when people show me their first wish list, I am struck by how many things are phrased in the negative. It seems they can tell me what they *don't* want. They don't want to fight with their teenagers, they don't want to have to work so hard, they don't want to have a wardrobe full of nothing to wear, they don't want to be overweight, in debt, always short of time …. the list goes on. Knowing what you don't want is useful and it can be the catalyst needed for change and in some ways it's a better place to be than 'denial' (although more painful to be in at the time) but this is no use to us when it comes to Cosmic Ordering. You see, the Universe has a hard time dealing with negatives.

Exercise: Thinking in the Negative

For the next 30 seconds, try **not** to think of a pink elephant.

Did you manage it? - I doubt it. Even if you've heard that example before, and quickly said to yourself 'Blue bunny, blue bunny, blue bunny' to try and override your natural urge to picture a pink elephant, I very much doubt you were quick enough and a pink elephant was *exactly* what you saw in your mind's eye - if only for a few seconds.

And this is the problem: if we focus on what we don't want, we may actually find we are attracting more of it.

Exercise: Phrasing Your Order in the Positive

Now I want you to choose one thing off your list and write it here, making sure that it is phrased in the positive. Remember; always ask for what you *do* want - not for what you *don't*.

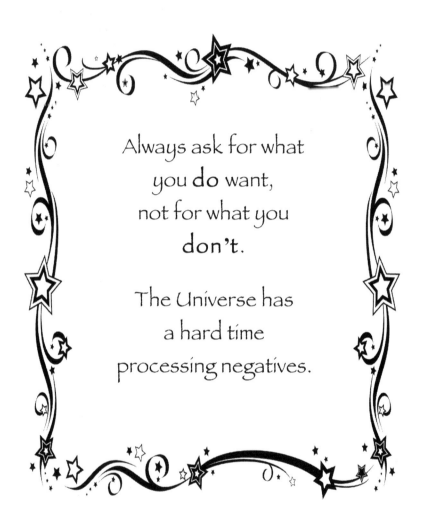

Always ask for what
you **do** want,
not for what you
don't.

The Universe has
a hard time
processing negatives.

Identifying Your Limiting Beliefs

Do you talk to yourself? Not necessarily out loud, just in your head. There, did you hear it? You talked to yourself right then about how much you talk to yourself!! You see, it never stops. We are constantly chatting away to ourselves. Much of what we say is drivel, much of it negative and contained within its repertoire are all your limiting beliefs.

Where did they come from originally? Doesn't really matter. Some come from parents, teachers, friends and the media. Some from perceived life experiences and some you created yourself. Doesn't really make a difference; the fact is that you have them and in many cases they are unconscious, that is we're not even aware that we have them or that we are saying them to ourselves dozens of times each day.

They govern how we act and what we say, they impact on the decisions we make and the habits we form and in the end they dictate what we have or don't have and who we are.

Now limiting beliefs are not all bad - in fact, they were designed for your safety. As a child you had experiences and you learnt that touching a stove was hot and not advisable and that falling off the edge of the sofa hurt and your limiting beliefs were formed. They literally set up your 'rules' about what you could do and what was not possible for you.

And the Problem is ...

Hopefully you're starting to see a problem here. Some of these limiting beliefs might be still useful to us, but many will be outdated now. What was important to protect a 5 year old (*'Don't talk to strangers'*) might be completely inappropriate to the 30 year old entrepreneur who's having a hard time making contacts at networking events. The trouble is these little devils have delusions of grandeur; they think they know best and in their desire to protect you they actually stifle you and your ability to create abundance. They affect who you are, the decisions you make, your habits and who and what you attract.

Limiting beliefs aren't always 'negative' beliefs though.

I'm going to call again here on my old friend and mentor - Zig Ziglar, whose talks I used to listen to on cassette back in the 90s. The whole tape was brilliant but this little story meant a lot to me back then, and even more to me now. I don't have the tape anymore but I tell the story often and it goes something like this:-

How to Train Fleas

Have you ever seen a Flea Circus? The little see-saw, the trampoline, the Ferris wheel all operated by tiny fleas? Well, a flea can jump over 6 feet, which is no good at all for the circus. But fleas can be trained and it's easier than you might think.

First put your fleas in a jar, just an ordinary jar, with tiny holes in the lid so that they can breathe. (You don't want to hurt the fleas, just train the fleas.)

To begin with it's very noisy as the fleas jump like crazy, trying to escape their tiny prison. They hit their heads on the inside of the lid over and over again, tat - tat - tat - tat- tat- tat. Come back in an hour and all is quiet. The fleas are fine, in fact they're still jumping, but they're not hitting their heads on the lid any more. They've trained themselves to jump within a millimetre of the lid so that they don't get hurt. Now you can remove the lid and the fleas are ready to join the circus. They will never jump any higher than the height of the lid of the jar because they believe that's as high as they can go - period.

And you and I are the same. Our lids are all at different heights but we all have them - loads of them. And when you really see them for what they are, most of them are imaginary. Some once had their origins in something real (like the jar lid was real for one hour for the fleas) but no longer have any relevance to who or where we are today. Some of them (often other people's opinions) never even had a basis in reality, someone just *told* you a lid was there and you believed them.

Gosh! I could write a whole book on limiting beliefs (and maybe one day I will), but for now all you need to successfully order is to identify them and be prepared to hold them to one side while you order.

'Until you make the unconscious conscious, it will direct your life and you will call it fate'

Carl G Jung.

I only just recently came across this quote. I was struggling to simplify this whole idea of the power limiting beliefs have over us and that identifying, naming and shaming them, is the key to diminishing their power - *especially* at the time of ordering. When explaining it to people on my Cosmic Ordering workshops I often liken the limiting beliefs to tiny, evil gremlins who can make themselves invisible in the dark and unexplained parts of your mind with invisibility cloaks and who, left to their own devices, would feed on your fears and doubts, running amuck, causing all sorts of untold damage and malfunctions. Some believe they mean well, and they will try and convince you that all they want to do is protect you - to keep you safe and free from harm and hurt, others are more sinister. But if you are keen to choose a life of growth and fulfilment, there are very few of them that really have your best interests at heart.

However, one thing the gremlins can't cope with is light. When you shine light (exploration) on them it makes them squirm. Trapped in the light's beam, their invisibility cloaks are rendered useless and then they become visible and you can see them for what they are. In other words, if you can identify them by name you diminish their power. Do it enough and they will 'poof' into thin air.

I really like that explanation, but it was long-winded and not very scientific so I wondered if someone might have come up with a shorter way to explain. I asked the Universe and this quote, which I'd never seen before, came right up to me when I lingered briefly on a page of a book I was flicking through, 'Soul Journey' by Lisa Cherry.

Huh - wouldn't you know it? That's *exactly* what I meant. Thank you Lisa and thank you Carl. In fact it's so good, let's hear it again......

'Until you make the unconscious conscious, it will direct your life and you will call it fate'

Carl G Jung.

107

Exercise: Naming Your Limiting Beliefs

So let's look at your 'order in waiting'. Go back to your wish list and the notes you made about any resistance you noticed. Are there any judgements you made about this request, the item, the process, the reactions of others, yourself, anything? And particularly note if you were reluctant to write it down. Hone the thought, delve deep - what's really going on? Why do you feel like that? What are your core beliefs about it?

Write whatever comes to mind here, don't skip on this - get curious, this matters. This is your life we're talking about. Try not to get caught up in blame or shame doing this exercise, just notice. Remember, it's not so important right now where you got these beliefs from and whose fault it is that you have them. Just recognise that you do and name them as specifically as you can.

_____

_____

_____

_____

_____

_____

_____

_____

_____

_____

_____

_____

_____

_____

And if you haven't read it already, now would be a good time to go back and read **Chapter 2 - The Day the Penny Dropped - The £10k and the £5k Story.**

OK, so now you have an order, phrased in the positive, and you're aware if you have any limiting beliefs attached to it (and we know you have, otherwise you'd already have it). So, what we need to do now is...

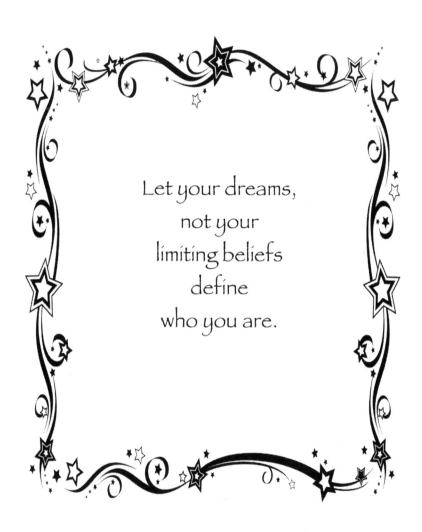

Let your dreams,
not your
limiting beliefs
define
who you are.

Be Specific - Be Very Specific

If I was sitting with you now, I'd want to help you be very specific about what you really want. See **Chapter 4 - The 'Just What I Asked For Stories'** to see the consequences of being sloppy in this area.

If it's something tangible, think about the size, colour, function, etc. but don't worry if you don't know *all* the details (and this is where I find Cosmic Ordering is different from goal setting).

I'll explain. Let's say what you *want* is a new car. Goal setting would say, go out and look at cars, collect brochures, take a test drive, choose your make, model, payment plan, put a picture of that make and model on your fridge and look at it every day.

Cosmic Ordering needs only that you know what you *want*. For example, *'a hatchback, metallic royal blue, new, comfortable to drive - dashboard that fits around you like a glove, cup holders in the centre panel, light grey quality fabric interior, room in the back for your dog cage and two suitcases, something that says successful but fun and individual and suits you perfectly. With the indicators on the right and windscreen wipers on the left. With a number plate that suits you and is significant in a good way - 56 or more miles to the gallon and environmentally friendly and with a low insurance group'.*

That way you don't have to go looking (unless you really want to) - the Universe knows what you want and will find the best match possible for you.

I'll give you another quick example. I once wanted a new top and in an attempt to be specific I asked for it to be, among other things, a size 14.

The top came within a couple of hours - a neighbour brought over a top (brand new) that she'd bought a few months earlier that didn't fit her and she thought I'd like it. It was exactly what I'd ordered - including it was a size 14. But guess what? - It didn't fit me either. It was tight on the arms and too short - how disappointing. It seems I'm not a 14 in all makes and designs after all!!

The next time I put an order in for clothes I was careful to say instead *'to fit me perfectly'* and from that day on, they always have. Some have been a size 14, some not, one was even a size 12 - which I might have rejected had I not *known* it would fit perfectly because I'd asked it to. (But more on accepting orders later).

For now, just know it's almost impossible to be too specific. But think about what you really want. Do you *really* want George Clooney or do you want *'a gorgeous smile, someone who will make you laugh, treat you with respect, has their own home/teeth/dog etc. etc?'* I hope you get the picture.

And talking of pictures...

Use Visualisation to 'Try it on for Size'

Projecting yourself forward in your mind's eye to the day you achieve a goal is a great thing to do. Imagine how it would feel. What can you see? What can you hear? How do others around you react? It can be very motivational and it can provide you with the drive for taking the necessary but often challenging steps towards its fruition. But it can also be an enormously useful tool for Cosmic Ordering too. Trying your order on for size, seeing it as if it has already arrived, will help you with your specifics. I have often modified my order after literally *'seeing'* some useful and important detail I may have entirely overlooked if I hadn't played the whole thing through.

And occasionally I've realised that's not what I want at all and I've saved myself the effort of ordering, only to find out after it's arrived.

It's also very enlightening in the limiting beliefs department. As you visualise, be sure to notice how you feel, how having, being, doing this 'ask' changes things. See and hear other people's reactions: they may not all be positive and may hold the key to why you haven't had or done it before.

Make a note of all you observe and if you decide to order you will have useful insights to help you hold those limiting beliefs to one side. Or maybe you can modify your order to get all you want but also minimise any undesirable outcomes.

It's in your hands and knowledge here is power.

Exercise: Getting Specific

Use this space to wordsmith your order until you are confident that it's accurate and specific. Once you are happy with it, project yourself forward in your mind and visualise how things will be after its arrival. Take your time, see, hear, feel and experience life after your order. Make notes of any specifics you've omitted and any further limiting beliefs that surface.

_____

_____

_____

_____

_____

_____

_____

_____

_____

_____

OK I think you're ready to place your order. Excited? You should be...

——— ✦✦✦ ———

To test whether you
really want something
before you order,

'jump into it'
for a while in your
mind and try it
on for size.

11

How to Place Your Order

So now you're ready to place your order and the important thing here is *clarity*. And clarity involves two key things: the right state of mind, and precise and accurate wording. Let's look at these two keys separately...

What is the right state of mind?

The best way I can describe this is to think of an analogue radio. Imagine all the music, all the sports news, all the show hosts' banter, all the interviews, plays, adverts for all the channels in the world are all *'out there'* at the same time, but when you tune the radio in to just the right frequency the radio can hear that single message crystal clear.

Our minds are often like that radio in the fiddling stage, flitting around from channel to channel, half conversations, random thoughts, replays of past events, pre-plays of up and coming events, flashes of images, faces, to do lists - sound familiar?

And I can empathise with you in this challenge. I'd love to tell you I have obtained a still and tranquil mind; that I can control my thoughts; that I am the master of my inner voice. I am, most certainly, not. In fact, I'm possibly one of the most butterfly-brained people I know; a consummate multi-tasker (if there really is such a thing). And actually I love that. I really like who I am and how I think. But I also understand that it's a rubbish state of mind for Cosmic Ordering. To put a successful order in, we need to be in that moment fully (if only for that moment). There, and nowhere else.

How you are 'in that moment' can vary from person to person, moment to moment. Personally, I've been fascinated, curious, content, absorbed, focused, inspired, contemplative, reflective, frustrated - although I wouldn't particularly recommend that last one. (See Chapter 4 - *The 'Two Cars off the Drive by Christmas' Story*).

What matters is that you are *'in the moment'*.

Where you are matters less, although for a short while I did think there was something significant about being in the shower (read Chapter 2 - *'The Day the Penny Dropped'* and you'll understand why). But now I understand its significance was mostly to do with the fact it was a ritualistic opportunity I'd created for myself where I reflected on things and, because I couldn't do much else in there but think, the distractions were minimal, which is very important with a mind like mine. I have since found it's possible to achieve that state of mind almost anywhere. It takes practice though, and in the beginning you can help yourself a great deal by finding a quiet, comfortable space where you feel good and can be confident of being undisturbed. Experiment until you find somewhere that works best for you. A bit like walking around with an indoor aerial for an old TV set until you find the best reception, no doubt certain places will have better energies that will assist you to 'tune in' too.

How to Word Your Order

By now, the bulk of your order is already written. You'll have written a list that states exactly what you want. You'll have described it in the positive and detailed the important aspects if it's a more complex 'ask'. You may have even given it a time frame, if that's important to you, or you may have left that open - your choice. But at the moment that's all you have. The shopping list is not your order.

You must <u>ask</u> for it.

The Bible says: *'Ask and you shall receive,'* not *'Write a list and you shall receive.'*

What you say to introduce your order is up to you. The phrase I use is: *'What I **really** want is...'*

I put a good deal of emphasis on the word *'really'*. I like the phrase, it sounds natural to me as if I'm talking to a real person. (Some of my clients actually do imagine they're talking to a real person, perhaps someone in a contact centre who puts your order on the system or a warehouse manager at a huge depot who jumps on a forklift truck to pick your order. Honestly, whatever works for you. Angels, spirits, goblins, fairies, it doesn't matter what you picture. That's just our human form needing to make sense of something that is way beyond our comprehension. And whatever works for you is what works for you. It's all good.)

I'm not so flexible about the next bit. In fact, I'd go so far as to say that this next bit is **non-negotiable**. You absolutely *must* finish your order with *'for the good of all concerned.'* Otherwise you are not likely to be happy with your results. (See Chapter 3 - *The 'For the Good of All Concerned' Stories* for what can happen if you forget.)

In fact, I feel it's *so* important, that I asked Anna Watkins, who painted 'Cosmic Dreams' for the book cover, to imprint the words *'For the good of all concerned'* on the canvas before she started painting. Take a look at how the painting developed on my website (www.Ellen-Unlimited.com) and you will see. You can't see the words now, but I know they're there.

And now, so do you!

Plan the words for your first order here:-

And now write your actual order, exactly as you are going to say it:-

Opening statement:-

Specifics of the Order:-

Any conditions: - Time frame, price, etc

_____

_____

_____

_____

_____

_____

_____

Closing Statement: - *'for the good of all concerned'*.

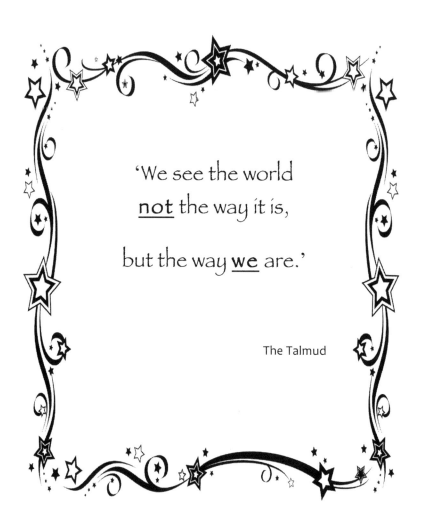

'We see the world **<u>not</u>** the way it is,

but the way **<u>we</u>** are.'

The Talmud

12

How to Recognise Your Order

Now that your order is placed, try to relax. Don't worry about it; carry on as normal with the calm, quiet reassurance that your order *will* come. Allow yourself to become expectant and enjoy the thrill of how and when the Universe will deliver. Be prepared for the miracle. Have faith.

The Bible tells us in Matthew 17 that *'If you had faith, even as small as a mustard seed, you could say to a mountain, "Move from here to there," and it would move. Nothing would be impossible.'*

Your order may be delivered to you in a variety of ways (couriers if you like, or some people call them channels). Some orders will literally arrive in your lap, no effort required; others will come as hunches and many will come as leads or 'clues'. For examples of these and what to look for, read Chapters 7, 8 and 9.

The first ones are pretty hard to miss and are dealt with in the next chapter - *'How to Receive Your Order'* - but the latter ones can be trickier to spot if you're not geared up to recognise them.

Your Reticular Filter

What I'm talking about here is activating your reticular filter. Your reticular filter or R.A.S. (Reticular Activated System) is a small, but very important part of your brain.

The word reticular just means net-like (a reticulated python is so called because it has a pretty net-like pattern on its back).

Think of your reticular filter like a fishing net. Some things will go through the holes and some will get caught in the net. (It all depends on how big your holes are and what you're trying to catch!) The best way to describe it though, is how it works in real life.

Exercise: Recognising your Reticular Filter at Work

I want you to imagine you have a brother. You go to see him and he's just bought a brand new car. You've never seen that make or model before, but you make a fuss of it. You admire the paint work, smell the leather and go out for a test drive in it.

The next day you are out walking or driving and you see first one, then another, then another of the same car. Three!!? What a coincidence you should see three!! And the very next day after seeing your brother's!!

Of course, the reality there is obvious. Five could have passed you the day before, but they weren't important to you then and so you didn't see them.

Make some notes here, about other examples that you've experienced.

You see, if you paid equal attention to every little bit of stimulus around you, you would literally go mad with overwhelm, so your reticular system filters out much of the world around you so you can concentrate on what's important. But who decides what's important? You do. Or rather your unconscious mind does and here's where it gets a little complicated.

Your reticular filter unconsciously makes your conscious mind only aware of things that your conscious mind has previously programmed your unconscious mind to be important.

Did you get that?

They discovered it - they, being the scientists who care about such things - in maternity wards. How come a new mother could sleep through any amount of noise, including other babies crying, but when her baby cried she woke up? The answer was clear. When the baby was born the first thing it did was cry. Now each human voice is unique. No one has ever lived, lives now or will ever live again that has exactly the same voice as you. So *that* sound is put on the mother's reticular filter and as the unconscious mind never sleeps, from that moment on whenever her baby cries she will wake up! Amazing!

The Moon Walking Bear Experiment

I've always been a big fan of Richard Wiseman - or rather, his 'Moon Walking Bear' experiment. You may have heard of it.

In it, a room of people are asked to watch a video of a basketball match. There are two teams, one dressed all in white, the other all in black. The audience is asked to count how many times the white team passes the ball and the video begins. It only lasts for about 30 seconds and the ball is passed back and forth across the screen as the players bounce and dodge and pass. It's quite tricky to keep your eye on the ball at times, but most people manage to count there are thirteen passes between members of the white team and they are correct. The audience are pleased with themselves but then the facilitator asks: *'And who saw the moon walking bear?'* The audience laughs, *'Bear? What bear - where?'*

The facilitator explains that during the video a man dressed in a black bear costume entered on the right, waved and then moon walked through the players before exiting on the left.

The audience think he is having a laugh. How could they possibly not notice a moon walking bear? But after much ridicule of the facilitator, the video is played again and there he is, large as life!! He walks and waves and moon-walks, and not in a sneaky way - it's absolutely incredible.

The first time I saw this iconic piece of work I was on the receiving end and I was absolutely convinced there must be two separate videos and that I was being 'tricked' to make a point. But I have shown that video to many others now. Take a look for yourself - I've put the link at the back of this book in the reference section. He's big, he's real and he's there for a good part of the video and no one sees him while they're counting the white team passes. Incredible!

So I've known about the dancing bear for years but actually didn't know it was Richard Wiseman until quite recently. I've talked about reticular filters in my coaching, goal setting and sales training but when I came to write this book I found another piece of interesting Richard Wiseman research. Somehow I'd been given the lead to watch a YouTube video called 'The Amazing Colour Changing Card Trick'. I'm not going to spoil that one for you. Again, I've put the link at the end of this book for you. Take a look for yourself and see if you can tell me how it's done!

Anyway, while I was watching that video, I noticed a gorilla suit in the background and it reminded me of the moon walking bear. 'Could it be the same guy?' I thought. So I Googled him and that's how I found the bear on YouTube.

A few days later, I was researching Barbel Mohr. I'd just discovered that as well as being the person who had first used the term 'Cosmic Ordering' in her book 'The Cosmic Ordering Service', she had also been the very person that Tracy had heard speak at the Mind, Body and Spirit Show in London a few days before Tracy made lunch for me at her house and this journey really took off.

Barbel's teaching had inadvertently been a huge piece in the puzzle for me and now I was writing my own book, I was curious to learn a little more about her, so I could reference her and her work in my book. I also had thoughts about contacting her when the book was finished to make sure she was happy with what I was putting out there. I somehow thought she would really appreciate the serendipity of how it had all come together.

I found that Barbel had written many books on Cosmic Ordering since her first one and I was curious to read them to see if we outlined the same lessons. I was sure we would have much in common. I decided, however, *not* to read any of her work before I'd finished writing mine as I didn't want to copy, either consciously or unconsciously, anything that she had done.

In the end though, I couldn't resist buying one of her books, 'The 21 Golden Rules of Cosmic Ordering'.

I figured I had about twenty or so little lessons I'd learnt over the years and at that point I'd listed them all as potential chapter headings and my curiosity got the better of me. Wouldn't it be funny if Barbel's twenty one were exactly the same as mine? (Actually I was more than a little worried they might be *exactly* the same and worse still that I was missing one!! I really needed to know that they weren't and that I wasn't.)

So when Barbel's book arrived, I quickly flicked through the chapter titles with the intention of putting the rest of the book away to read later when my book had gone off to the proof-reader. And for the most part, that's exactly what I've done. But my eye fell on a name just a few pages in ….. Richard Wiseman!!! Oh no, I thought, what a coincidence that I should see Richard Wiseman's name here just a few days after I'd found out he was the man behind the moon walking bear exercise and my reference for my bit about reticular systems (I really hope you're getting the irony here?) I just couldn't resist knowing more, I was desperate to understand why Barbel had chosen to reference him and it made fascinating reading.

In a nutshell, Barbel tells of a study that Richard had carried out where he looked for people who described themselves either as 'lucky devils' or 'jinxes'. He then carried out an experiment with both groups of people. First, he showed them the moon walking bear video. The results from the two groups were remarkably similar - very few people noticed the bear. I love the way Barbel explains this: 'It's simple,' she says. 'No one ordered a moon walking bear.'

Then the two groups were each given a page from a newspaper and asked to count the number of images on the page. In the middle was a huge advertisement with the following message: '*You will win £100 if you tell your tester that you have seen this advert.*'

Almost all of the lucky devils saw the advert and won the money, while almost none of the jinxes did. They were all too busy counting the images and overlooked the advert. Like the bear, they just didn't see it. Of course there is a thought that some of them *might* have seen it but then thought it was a joke, a trick, or just too good to be true and so they didn't tell their tester in case they were wrong, judged, looked foolish etc. Different problem (and it's more to do with the next chapter, Chapter 13 - How to Receive Your Order), but the result is the same - no £100 for the jinxes!

Amazing, huh? I think that just makes my point better than anything else I can imagine. Your order will come, but listen for the door bell and if you get a hunch that you need to be somewhere, ring someone or read something then do it. Put yourself out there. I often say the postman knocks three times and what I mean by that is if I hear or see something three times from three different sources I've learnt to check it out.

Keep your eyes and ears and most importantly your mind open to the infinite possibilities and messages around you. Expect what you ordered to arrive and not only will you attract it to you, but you will recognise it when it does.

Notes:-

Sadly, during my research, I learned that Barbel passed away suddenly in 2010. I am deeply saddened to think that she and I will not meet in person and that the world has lost such an inspirational leader. But her husband, Manfred, continues to promote her work and because of that, she will live on through her books. When I have finished writing 'Cosmic Ordering Made Easier' and it has finally left my hands for the publisher, I look forward to buying her books and 'meeting' her in this way at least.

Be on your guard
for resistance.

Ask yourself 'what is
my issue with this?

Is this resistance
or is this wrong?'

13

How to Receive and Keep Your Order

Maybe you're thinking to yourself right now, how hard can it be? Surely you just say 'thank you very much'? Well yes, in an ideal world that's *exactly* what you would do, but we're not in an ideal world and it's amazing how many people don't.

We all know people who come into a little extra money and then almost immediately that they have an unexpected crisis that uses up their windfall. New tyres, a leaky cistern, an emergency trip needed - complete with a tankful of petrol, and they find themselves right back at square one.

Or they get promoted and then have issues with their new boss or their hours or they suddenly have some crisis at home and they decide to leave or go back to their old role.

Or they find their dream house and it all looks perfect and such a good price and then there are complications, their buyer pulls out or someone gazumps them and they may lose it. Or they might eventually get it but they will end up paying a lot more for it.

Or they get offered the most wonderful opportunity to do something - a business opportunity or walking the Great Wall of China for charity, the chance to go a TV game show - and consciously they believe they're really looking forward to it, but as the day approaches they become sick or they fall and sprain their ankle so they can't go.

Or after several years alone they finally attract a really perfect partner but they keep pushing them away and mistrusting them until that lovely new partner finally gives up and walks away, leaving them alone again.

Or they finally start to lose weight and they join a gym and they're doing so well, they're nearly at their goal and then - bang - they break a leg or slip a disc and they can't exercise and now they have the perfect excuse for the weight to creep back on again where it was comfortable.

It's all symptoms of the same thing really. It's unconscious self-sabotage, and it's all thanks to these damn limiting beliefs again, creeping back in and spoiling things. Often referred to in the corporate world as the 'Peter Principle*', we get ourselves back to where we feel we belong - in line with our self image and the 'level' (or limit) that comes with it.

This is where work like affirmations, NLP (Neuro Linguistic Programming) and hypnotherapy can be useful to re-programme deep seated core beliefs that manage our expectations. It can be useful to employ the services of a therapist, coach or hypnotherapist to work on these habitual thinking patterns with you. For most of us though, awareness is the key - noticing resistance when it occurs and seeing it for what it is.

Resistance is Futile.

It's just your limiting beliefs trying to protect you. Notice, observe and listen to what they have to say, give them your full attention, but just for a moment. (A little respectful and undivided attention now, could prevent them from having a 'hissy fit' later to get your attention and then they could really do some damage!)

You see, a lot of times that's all they ask for. They want you to hear them out and give their concerns some consideration. After all, in their mind, they're only trying to protect you and keep you from harm's way. And sometimes there's a seed of concern worth noting, but often they're just afraid of change and growth and after hearing them out and, again, seeing them for what they are, you can let them go and carry on with accepting and enjoying your order because you don't need them anymore.

Another useful antidote to limiting beliefs getting in the way of saying 'yes please' to your order is gratitude. Gosh, I could write a whole book just on gratitude (and maybe one day I will), but I've found a grateful heart is an accepting heart and the Universe does seem to appreciate being appreciated (oh, and let's face it, who doesn't?)

Think about it for a moment - think about giving someone something as simple as a compliment:

> 'What a lovely dress,' you say. The recipient of your attention squirms uncomfortably and says:

> 'What, this old thing? I've had it for years. It should have gone to the charity shop years ago really - just look at the state of this hem!'

OK, so I exaggerate for effect, but I bet, like me, you've had similar conversations before and I suspect, like me, you thought 'Gosh, that was hard work - I wish I hadn't bothered!' and you'll think twice next time before complimenting them again.

By contrast, imagine the person whose eyes light up as they say 'Thank you - that's so kind of you to notice!'

How does that feel?

Well it seems the Universe is the same. It appreciates gratitude and I've noticed that the people who are grateful and appreciate what they have are not only happier people but they attract more and more of the same.

Here's a gem of wisdom for you: 'Cosmic Ordering means you can have what you want, but real happiness comes from wanting what you have.' And yes - you can have both. That's what gratitude will do for you.

Exercise: Developing Your Gratitude Muscle

Like most things you can develop your capacity for gratitude with practice. Here's a small but very powerful exercise that you can do every day that will really make a difference.

Each night before you go to bed, write down the three things that you were most grateful for today. It can be as small as a smile from a stranger, the laughter of a child, a dew drop on an exquisite rose, to incidental - you found your keys first time this morning, the kids ate their breakfast without bickering, to monumental - you got the job, the pay rise, the house!

By putting your gratitude into words, you will increase your appreciation and deepen your memory of these events too. Make it a rule not to go to bed until you have captured and reflected upon all three.

Have a go right now. What three things are you *most* grateful for so far today? Write them down here:-

I have been amazed at the transformational power of this tiny exercise in my own life. Firstly it creates perspective; what might have felt like a bad day is suddenly full of candidates for my 'Gratitude Top 3'. An already good day swells to epic proportions and wonderful memories are strengthened and deepened. Very often lessons are learnt in the reflection time about how to create more of the same and hunches for contacts and actions can occur too. (Be sure to write those down) And finally, and most wonderfully, I find that during the day as little incidents occur, I am mentally noting them as candidates for that night's list and so my reticular filter becomes on the look-out for 'all things good' and it should be no surprise to you that because of that, I spot more and more good things each day.

*The Peter Principle was formulated by Dr. Laurence J. Peter and Raymond Hull in their 1969 book 'The Peter Principle', a humorous look at the thought that we all work to a hierarchy of our own design and that we will all only rise to our own perceived level of incompetence.

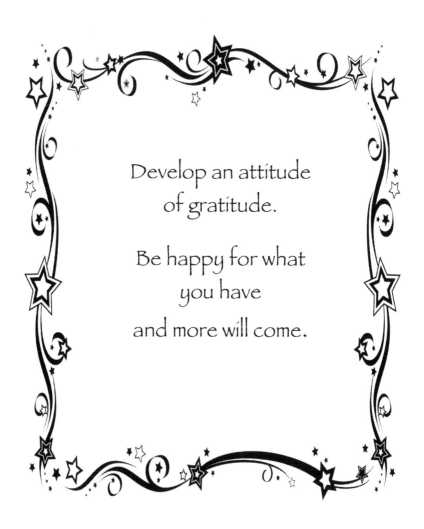

Develop an attitude
of gratitude.

Be happy for what
you have
and more will come.

14

Frequently Asked Questions

Q. Do I have to order in the shower?

> **A.** No, not at all. That was where I had my first real breakthrough, and as a result of that, it's still one of my favourite places. But I now regularly order in the garden, over the fields with my horses, out walking the dogs and even in the car (passenger side, of course). And you will find *your* best places too, but for most people it's somewhere they can be still, calm, content, reflective, curious and, most importantly, undisturbed.

> For more information about getting into the right state of mind, see **Chapter 11 - How to Place Your Order.**

Notes:-

Q. Should I give my order a timeframe or deadline?

A. That's an interesting one, and I have to say many times I don't. But then, I'm very used to my orders arriving within a few hours. In fact, I feel a bit hard done by if they take longer than a day! However, there are occasions when the timing is important, for instance, the time when I was due to move my horses to their new yard.

The Story of the Missing Horse Trailer

After I moved to the beautiful village of Blunsdon, for a while my horses had to stay at my old yard just 8 miles down the road. I say *just* 8 miles because that didn't seem very far - until I started adding up the miles. 'There and back' was 16 miles. And 'there and back twice a day' was 32 miles and times that by 7 days and we have 224 miles a week!! Gosh - no wonder I felt like I was always filling up the petrol tank.

So I found a place in Blunsdon for my two girls (that's a whole other story. See **Chapter 6 - The 'Nothing is Impossible' Stories - The Story of the Perfect Pony Paddock**) and I was planning to transport them at the end of the month. Just a few days before the intended move, I found myself out in the field, brushing horses, and contemplating the fate of my horse trailer. There was nowhere really for me to store it at the new fields and, more to the point, I'd bought it in partnership with the lady who ran my current yard. If I kept it at my yard, *she* wouldn't have easy access and of course, vice versa. Neither of us was really in the position to buy the other out, so the sensible option was probably to sell the thing and split the money. The problem was it was getting on a bit and had definitely seen better days. It was hard to think that either of us would be able to get anything with our share of the money raised so I found myself thinking, *'What we could really do with is it getting stolen!! Then we'd get the insurance money which would probably be more than we'd get if we sold it.'* That was the Wednesday.

On the Thursday, I was chatting to Linda (the co-owner of said horse trailer) as we walked back from the fields to the stables via the yard car park. And as we talked, my eyes went past her to the empty space which should have been filled by our trailer. Yep, it was gone!! It had sat there happily for *four years* but one day after my saying it - it was stolen!

I hadn't really realised I'd put an order in - I'd been joking really, it was just a thought. But the Universe didn't know the difference; I'd said it exactly like an order.

Now, as it happens, I do believe that the Universe has a terrific sense of humour, but on this occasion it had taken me entirely on face value. And once I got over the shock I was delighted. It was actually a very good result, but I couldn't help but think *'After* I'd moved the horses' would have been a better ask. Just three more days! Now I had to put out an appeal for someone to transport me to my new fields. Yes, there are times when adding a date can be very useful indeed.

Notes:-

Keep a record of
your successes.

They will give you
the confidence
to ask
for bigger things.

Q. Should I write my order down?

A. For many years I have taught the importance of writing goals down as part of my management and leadership training programmes and to the dozens of individuals I've coached to help them reach their goals. There's a lot of sense in writing things down: it helps you become clearer, it helps you to be specific and all of the other lovely SMART* objectives, plus it has some evaluation built in.

The other really key reason for writing it down is it helps to activate your reticular filter, that small part of the brain that acts like a net. (See **Chapter 12 - How to Recognise Your Order** if you want to know more about your reticular filter or RAS.)

That said, apart from complex and multi-faceted asks that require me to list their components carefully, I don't write the majority of my orders down before I order them. Many are done *'in the moment'* as a result of some mental exploration about a problem, challenge, goal or just life that I'm experiencing at the time. And I suspect the same will be true for you. Mostly, these days I only write them down after they've arrived to help me keep a record of all my successes so that I will have more stories to tell for my coachees and on my workshops. It's also useful to have that list for times when things aren't flowing so well - you can look back on your past successes and it helps boost your belief in and gratitude for the Universe.

---

* The SMART in SMART Objectives, if you've not come across it before, stands for all the good things a well-formed objective should be: Specific, Measurable, Achievable, Realistic and Time-tabled.

Notes:-

_____

_____

_____

_____

_____

_____

Q. Should I be chanting the order several times in front of a mirror, morning and night?

> **A.** No, definitely not. What you are thinking of there are auto suggestions or affirmations. These are very useful in helping you re-programme your core beliefs but they are **not** your orders. Think of it like this: If you rang your local superstore with your order and then rang again every few minutes with the same order It's likely that the order clerk would suspect he's dealing with a slightly disturbed person and perhaps cancel the order altogether. No, put your order in once, clearly, specifically and definitely and then don't worry about it. It's in the system and **will** be delivered according to your instructions. See **Chapter 11 - How to Place Your Order.**
>
> But since you brought it up, let's talk about why affirmations can be useful.
>
> Affirmations can be phrases like:
>
> - Cosmic Ordering works for me.
>
> - My orders are always specific and clear.
>
> - I always find a car parking space.
>
> - All things happen for a reason and it serves me.
>
> - There is no failure only feedback.

- The Universe does not judge.

These are all useful phrases and I'm sure you can think of others specifically for yourself that you may wish to work on to overcome any old negative or limiting patterns.

The reason it's useful to repeat these phrases to ourselves is this is how the mind gets programmed. When we were children, our parents said similar phrases to us over and over again. Like grooves in an old LP record, the tracks were laid in. Then, as adults, we became in charge of our own computer keyboard but most of us never fully realise all the responsibility that comes with that but rather, we continue to 'replay' the old messages we heard growing up. There are a lot of excellent books covering the topic of affirmations and reprogramming and I have listed a few of my favourites for you in **Chapter 16 - Where Do I Go From Here?**

Notes:-

Don't give up.

You are a
'work in progress.'

We **all** are.

Q. I put an order in and it didn't come - should I put it in again?

> **A.** Well, this is a little harder for me to answer without knowing exactly what you asked for and what you said and did and how long you've been waiting. And this is why it can be useful to have me as a coach, so we can talk about those things and uncover your personal sticking points.
>
> On the whole, my first answer is to be patient. Give it some time, stay vigilant, reflect over events since you ordered - have you missed anything? Next, look at your order - could it have been improved upon? Once you're satisfied it's definitely not coming, re-craft it and put a new order in. To help you with these reflections, here are just a few of the possible causes why an order might not arrive .. .. ..

- You didn't *really* want it.

- You weren't specific enough.

- You were not 'in the moment' when you ordered.

- You have *unconscious* limiting beliefs that blocked your order (you will need to find and name them).

- You didn't phrase it in the positive (the Universe can't deliver negatives).

- It *did* turn up, but not in the way you were expecting so you didn't recognise it and it went away again. In other words, the delivery driver knocked at your door and you denied all knowledge of the delivery.

Notes:-

Q. Can I Cosmic Order for someone else?

A. I get asked this one a lot; husbands for wives and vice versa, mothers for children and *'for my poor friend who... ... ...'*

And always my answer is this:

You can. And I believe there's absolutely no harm in asking for good things for the people you love, for the good of all concerned. *However,* before you rush off to save the world, are you so sure that you really, really know their minds? Can you be absolutely confident that that's what they want for themselves? I'm not so sure. And even if by chance you were absolutely spot on with your order, you may still be setting yourself (and them) up for disappointment, because if their core beliefs around the subject are limiting (and let's face it, that's highly likely, given that you feel compelled to help them) they may not accept it when it comes.

In other words, my advice to you is to concentrate on yourself, work on what *you* need and want and let others work on themselves - when they're ready. The interesting upshot of this approach is that often when these other people see the spectacular changes in you as you align yourself to receive more of what you want, they will often become curious and inspired to know more and then you can gently open the door for them to learn to do it for themselves. Try leaving this book lying around where they might come across it. Or you could try a less subtle approach and buy them their own copy for a birthday or Christmas present.

Notes:-

Q. If Cosmic Ordering's so great, where's my million?

A. Do you know, if I'd collected £1 from everyone who asked this question, I think I'd be well on my way to *my* first million!

If you've read the book, you know the answer. If like me, you like to shortcut the system and you've come straight to the F.A.Q. section at the back, looking for the quick answers, then I'm sorry to disappoint you with this one. *Cosmic Ordering is the shortcut.* And you can't shortcut the shortcut …… **Now read the book!!!!**

(Big clue for the really impatient ones - the answer to this question starts in **Chapter 2 - *The Day the Penny Dropped.*)**

Notes:-

Q. What if I get just what I asked for, but it's not what I wanted?

A. This will undoubtedly happen as you fine tune your asking skills. It still happens to me sometimes. I've learnt it's OK to simply reject the order (please do this nicely, *especially* if it involves someone else), and then put a revised order in for what you really *do* want. You'll get better the more you do.

In the meantime, I suggest reading **Chapter 4 - The 'Just What I Asked For' Stories** where you'll gain valuable insights into how the Universe interprets your order and that might help you realise where your order was flawed.

I also recommend reading **Chapter 10 - How to Prepare Your Order** again. Here you'll find tips on being more specific so that what you ask for is exactly what you want. And you'll be more delighted with your results.

Notes:-

Q. What do I do if I forget to say 'For the good of all concerned'?

A. I really hope that with all of the references that I've made in this book you do **not** forget. But if you do realise that you have forgotten, then my suggestion to you is to cancel the order and put a fresh one in with *'for the good of all concerned'* included just as soon as possible. And don't do it again!

Notes:-

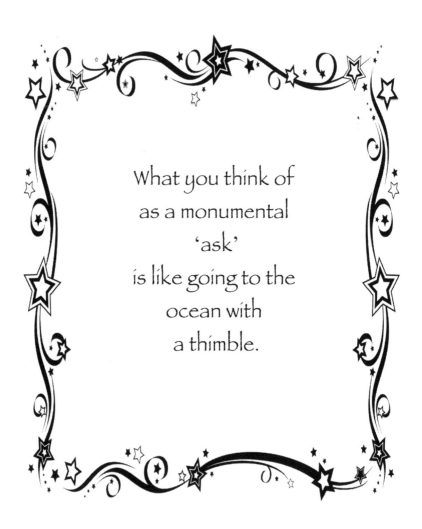

What you think of
as a monumental
'ask'
is like going to the
ocean with
a thimble.

15

In a Nutshell

Step 1 - Preparing Your Order (Chapter 10)

Remember, before you place a Cosmic Order it's worth taking the time to do a little preparation. Be sure to:-

- ❖ Keep it positive. Ask for what you want, not for what you **don't** want.

- ❖ Be specific - very specific.

- ❖ Don't worry if you think it's possible or not - that's not your concern.

- ❖ Only ask for the **what** and let the Universe deal with the **how**.

- ❖ Test out your 'ask' by visualising it already received and try it on for size.

- ❖ Include a timeframe or date if it's important to your order (remember the horse trailer story in 'FAQ - *Should I give my order a timeframe or deadline?*').

- ❖ Identify and name any limiting beliefs you have that might get in the way of your ordering, recognising or receiving your order.

Notes:-

Step 2 - Placing Your Order (Chapter 11)

This is the easy part and involves just three simple elements:-

1. **Get in the right state of mind.** The real key is that you are totally 'in the moment'.

2. **Hold your limiting beliefs to one side.** If you name them they'll have no real power to stop you.

3. **Ask for what you want 'for the good of all concerned'.** Please always remember to add that phrase to the end of every order.

Notes:-

Step 3 - Recognising Your Order (Chapter 12)

Your only job now is to put yourself in the position to receive your order and to stay alert. Get to work. Notice any **hunches** you have about places you need to be or people you need to call and do them. Spot things that are out of the ordinary; these are **leads - follow them.** Have fun!! It's so exciting seeing how your order will come.

Notes:-

Step 4 - Receiving Your Order (Chapter 13)

Once your order has been delivered it's up to you to receive it. Be willing to say **'Yes'** to the Universe. Make it easy for the Universe to deliver to you.

Notice any resistance that you have if you feel you're pushing something away or making it difficult. Examine it carefully to see if it's valid. If it is, proceed with caution, and if it's not, go ahead and accept your order.

Finally, express gratitude for all the gifts you receive - and you will open the doors for even more good things to come to you in the future.

Notes:-

_____

_____

_____

_____

_____

_____

_____

_____

_____

_____

In all things,
it is not important
that you progress
slowly,

it is only important
that you don't
stop.

16

Where Do I Go From Here?

I hope you found that short *'Aide-mémoire'* useful. However, if you need any more depth in any of these areas, simply refer to the appropriate chapters and get studying.

And if you can't find the answers you need there, take a look on my website **www.Ellen-Unlimited.com** where I'll be regularly adding more hints & tips. You can sign up for my newsletter there too.

If you have lots of questions or just want to learn more about Cosmic Ordering, then you might also want to consider coming to one of my **'Cosmic Ordering Made Easier' workshops** or having a **one to one coaching session** with me on Skype. You'll find details of both of these options on my website too.

Of course, the very best way to learn and to get better at anything is to have a go - and as long as you remember to say *'For the good of all concerned'*, what's the worst that can happen?

Nothing!

That's right - **'Nothing' is the worst that can happen!**

So go on - have a go, and don't forget to keep a journal. Recording your successes, and your lessons, will help build your skills and your confidence to go for even more of what you want in the future.

Good luck!

(The definition of L.U.C.K - Labouring Under Correct Knowledge).

Further Reading & Resources

The following books are all on my bookshelf here in my office - some are very old friends that I have read many times over and can recommend with confidence, others are hot-off-the-press and await my attention, but I believe will be of great value.

Further reading on and around Cosmic Ordering -

- The Cosmic Ordering Service - Barbel Mohr
- The 21 Golden Rules of Cosmic Ordering - Barbel Mohr
- Positively Happy - Noel Edmonds
- The Power of Intention - Dr. Wayne W. Dyer
- Spiritual Serendipity - Richard Eyre
- The Celestine Prophesy, an Adventure - James Redfield

On Overcoming Limiting Beliefs & Thriving -

- Soul Journey - Lisa Cherry
- How to Heal Your Life - Louise L Hay
- Feel the Fear & Do It Anyway - Susan Jeffers
- What to Say When You Talk to Yourself - Shad Helmstetter

On Positive Thinking, Success and Achieving Your Goals -

- Think and Grow Rich - Napoleon Hill
- The Strangest Secret - Earl Nightingale
- The Purpose of Your Life - Carol Adrienne
- The 7 Habits of Highly Effective People - Stephen R. Covey
- Awaken the Giant Within - Anthony Robbins
- The Charge - Brendon Burchard

YouTube links demonstrating your reticular filter in action -

- Richard Wiseman's Colour Changing Card Trick ~
  www.youtube.com/watch?v=voAntzB7EwE
- Richard Wiseman's Moon Walking Bear ~
  www.youtube.com/watch?v=UfA3ivLK_tE

Conclusion

I wasn't sure this book needed a conclusion at first, but now, as I come to the end, I find there's something I'd *really* like to say to you...

Just after the whole Cosmic Ordering thing got out of the closet in May this year (2012), New College in Swindon booked me to run a series of Cosmic Ordering Made Easier workshops for them. The course blurb went in their autumn prospectus and shortly after, a man apparently emailed them and ranted about my course (and a few other similarly themed titles), asking if this was how his council tax was now being spent - '*to fund this sort of nonsense*'.

The organiser at New College was not at all perturbed by such an onslaught and no doubt wrote a courteous, but professional reply. But I reflected on this man's opinion for some time after she'd told me about it.

Initially, before I wrote this book, I had been frightened that I might receive that very reaction from some people and that they would think that what I was doing was somehow trite, shallow, 'away with the fairies' and detached from the real horrors and heartaches of the world and I didn't want to be thought of that way.

But now I've actually been faced with my first attack, I know I'll be fine. Because I had this thought and I ask you to explore the same thought with me now and see what *you* think:-

Can you imagine a world where everyone could Cosmic Order successfully? Where everyone understood that there was enough for everyone and that they had at their fingertips all the love, support and wisdom they needed. That any lack was due to their own thoughts and limiting beliefs. And more over, that they alone had the power to overcome these barriers. Can you imagine what an amazing world that would be?

No, this is not 'trite' at all …… this is HUGE!!! To the point that, as I look back over the developments I've seen in this world, even in my short lifetime, things that were once seen as gimmicks or passing fads are often looked back on fondly as the beginning of a more advanced current technology and I wonder if this isn't just another point in our evolution. Somewhere we're all going together.

Maybe that's too grand, but honestly, who knows? But I do know it can only be for the good of all concerned. And for that I am enormously grateful.

———— ·❀❀· ————

The End

Believe in You

'Our deepest fear is not that we are inadequate.
Our deepest fear is that we are powerful beyond measure.
It is our light, not our darkness that most frightens us.

We ask ourselves,
'Who am I to be brilliant, gorgeous, talented, fabulous?'
Actually, who are you *not* to be?

You are a child of the Universe.
Your playing small does not serve the world.
There is nothing enlightened about shrinking so that
other people won't feel insecure around you.

We are all meant to shine, as children do.
We were born to make manifest the glory of
the Universe that is within us.
It's not just in some of us; it's in everyone.

And as we let our own light shine,
we unconsciously give other people permission to do the same.
As we are liberated from our own fear,
our presence automatically liberates others.'

Marianne Williamson from her book,
'A Return to Love - *Reflections on the Principles of A Course in Miracles*'

About the Author

Trainer ~ Coach ~ Mentor ~ Facilitator ~ Keynote Speaker ~ Writer

Ellen started her career over 30 years ago, first in retail management and management training and later in 'business to business' sales and sales management. In 1996, she formed **ElleRich Training Ltd** to provide local companies with training that made a real difference to their bottom line. She still specialises in **customer service and sales training**, plus all the **communication and management skills** needed to support them.

Her current portfolio of courses stands at over 50 topics of **business management, communication and leadership skills**. Her training style is always fun, interactive and motivational as well as informative and behaviour changing.

She has designed and delivered various courses, workshops, team building events, training road-shows and bespoke leadership and coaching/mentoring programmes to hundreds of organisations including **Marks & Spencer, Miele, Virgin Wines, Zurich, ARVAL PHH, Overdrive, BCA, Exploration Logistics, Pronuptia, SPATEX, WWT, British Gas, Texaco, npower, Aldi, Network Rail, The Marine Conservation Society and Direct Wines.**

Ellen has acquired her **Certificate in Training Practice** and for her special project she chose to study learning organisations and to develop competencies that could be used for benchmarking studies. She has studied **NLP and Accelerated Learning** as well as a variety of **personality profiling tools** and uses their lessons and insights to help organisations save time and money by aiding learners' attention, retention and skills transfer.

She also offers professional coaching and mentoring, and is asked to do so frequently for individuals who need special attention with things like leadership skills, presentation delivery, general business communication or confidence and credibility.

She studied **Performance Coaching for Business** with **Newcastle University** and **Coaching and Mentoring** with **Bath University in Swindon**. She has also been a volunteer mentor for their Women into Enterprise Scheme. In 2010 she added **ILM level 5 in Coaching & Mentoring** to her coaching qualifications. She is also a **High Growth Business Coach** for **Business South West's 'Solutions for Business' Programme**.

In the last 10 years, Ellen has also added keynote speeches and seminar work to her portfolio, with **NatWest and Lloyds TSB** inviting her to speak about **"Selling through Service"** to their Senior Business Managers at their monthly conferences. She has also been the key note speaker at **SPATEX,** the annual four day mega event for the whole of the pool and spa industry, for two years in a row. Ellen has been sponsored by **Barclays** and **Microsoft** as the featured speaker at several **Business Link** events, covering a whole range of business related topics. She is also an avid and enthusiastic networker and is a key member of **The Athena Group** in Swindon and a Premium Member and Connector for **Business Scene**.

Cosmic Ordering Made Easier: Although Ellen had been practising Cosmic Ordering herself for many years, the first time she mentioned it 'out loud' was at a Business Growth Show early in 2012 (now affectionately referred to as 'the day it got out of the closet') and things have moved at an epic pace ever since. She has found herself in great demand as a Cosmic Ordering coach and speaker and now runs her own '*Cosmic Ordering Made Easier*' workshops covering the material in this book as well as teaching the subject at New College, Swindon. '*Cosmic Ordering Made Easier*' is Ellen's first book, but she is already planning several more and looking forward to the challenge.

In her spare time, Ellen enjoys spending time with her husband Rich at their home on the edge of the Cotswolds with their two Rhodesian Ridgeback dogs, Merlin and Sumatra, and her New Forest Pony Meg. She and Rich are also part of the team of trustees who run the Rhodesian Ridgeback Welfare Trust (www.rrwt.org), a national charity that works to rescue, rehome and rehabilitate these beautiful dogs, which are sometimes referred to as Lion Hounds. Ellen is also a Zumba fan and tries hard never to miss her weekly class at the local village hall.

Contact Details

ElleRich Training Ltd:

> **Telephone:** 01793 709709 ~ **Email:** Ellen@ellerich.co.uk
> **Website:** www.ellerichtraining.co.uk ~ **Twitter** @ElleRichLtd

Cosmic Ordering Made Easier:

> **Website:** www.Ellen-Unlimited.com
> **Follow me on Twitter** @EllenUnlimited

Rhodesian Ridgeback Welfare Trust:

> **Website:** www.rrwt.org ~ **Email:** ellen.watts@rrwt.org
> **Facebook:** www.facebook.com/friendsofrrwt

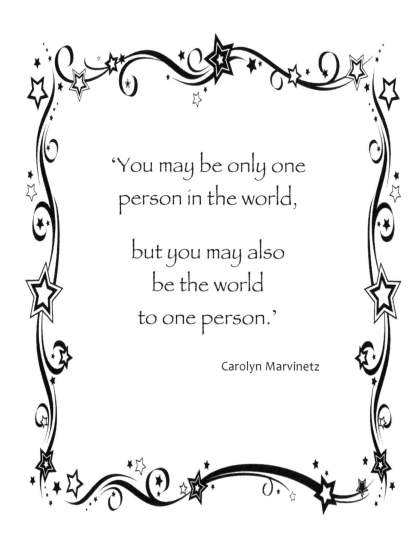

'You may be only one
person in the world,

but you may also
be the world
to one person.'

Carolyn Marvinetz

What People are Saying About Ellen Watts & her 'Cosmic Ordering Made Easier' Workshops

When I first met Ellen and learnt about Cosmic Ordering, I just wanted to learn more. I was really intrigued. Going to the workshop, Ellen gave detailed stories, information and tips. It was an amazing experience! Ellen is so understanding and helpful when discussing your orders and how to get them right. It's nice to know she's there on hand to help and guide you on your way. Ellen is an inspiration! I can't wait for the book!

Gemma Knott
Member of the '*I am a Writer*' Group

I knew there was something amazing about Ellen when we first met and was not surprised when she shared Cosmic Ordering with me. Working with Ellen on a 1-2-1 basis and in workshops has been an inspiration to me on a personal & professional level and I'm excited about my future orders coming in.

I've just finished reading 'Cosmic Ordering Made Easier' and I think it's great. It's just as if Ellen's speaking it to me, and exactly how she told me. I'm hooked and intrigued all over again. I love the opening on how to use the book, perfectly put to get the best from it.

Teresa McGrady
Network Marketing Professional

I love Ellen's warmth; she really wants you to enjoy life to the full. I can't recommend her coaching enough.

Mandie Cran
The Buzz Group

Ellen has an aura that draws you in and answers the questions in your head. I had a compelling need to sit down and speak with her the first time we met. I didn't even know I needed the 'Ellen Effect' but since meeting her and enlisting her as my mentor and coach, I haven't looked back. I've been able to achieve clarity in my business, and have benefited from the amazing insights that both Ellen and Cosmic Ordering can bring to a person's life. She is compelling, inspiring and right!

Holly Scott-Donaldson
Donaldson Marketing Bureau

I am writing to say how much I enjoyed the course last week. I learned a lot, not only about Cosmic Ordering but also about how we limit ourselves with our 'decisions' about what we could, or should, have in life.' The other people on the course also greatly enjoyed themselves and that made it all the more worth the journey.

Diana G Mawson PhD, C.Hyp
Clinical Hypnotherapist, Thought Field Therapist,
Trainer & Business Performance Coach

I found Ellen to be a very engaging and motivational speaker. I enjoyed the course much more than I'd even hoped and expected.

Tina Weatherley

Amazing
things happen
when a prepared person
and an
opportunity collide.

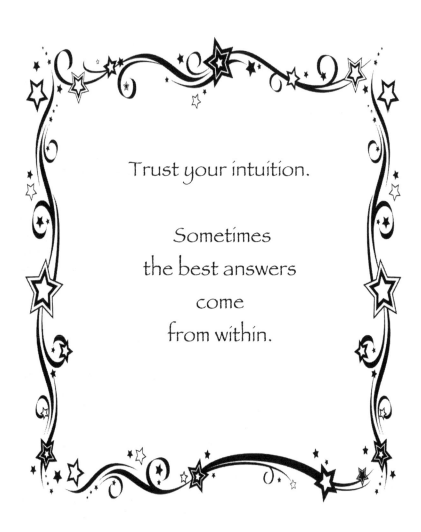

Trust your intuition.

Sometimes
the best answers
come
from within.

As a young child, I was aware of a magical realm or spiritual dimension where heartfelt wishes were answered and came true. But as soon as I went to school, a shutting-down process of my 'unlimited self' began in order to be accepted and conform.

But as we enter a new Golden Age in the evolution of humanity on 21st December 2012, I truly believe that, more than ever, the time is right for books like Ellen's to be published. This book will help guide those who want a taste of 'Heaven on Earth' to realise their own dreams and full potential, for the good of all concerned.

Briony Roberts
Director of Blue Bear Communications

Ellen Watts is an extraordinary person with an extraordinary talent for helping people achieve what they need and want in their lives. Her unique blend of Cosmic Ordering coaching with more traditional coaching and mentoring methods is highly potent, and it brings about truly fantastic results.

I am so grateful to the Cosmos for bringing Ellen into my life at the very moment I needed her. She has been an amazing catalyst for good things happening for me and I feel blessed to have her near me. My own Cosmic Ordering skills are still a 'work in progress' but I now know that it's my limiting beliefs which hold me back and have done so for so long. My sessions with Ellen have helped me to recognise and be aware of them, so now I am able to work on eradicating them in the future. Thank you, Ellen for the gift of you.

And I am so delighted that Ellen has written 'Cosmic Ordering Made Easier'. I really can hear her voice talking through the pages! I know this book will be so beneficial for so many more people than she can reach on a 1-1 basis. Her approach truly does work and this book will help create more of the happiness and contentment that so many people aspire to have in their lives.

Rachel Goddard
Regional Director for The Athena Network

I found your Cosmic Ordering course both informative and fun! How often do you get given the rules and structure to ask for what you want? I have had some successes and I am now ordering bigger!!

Ellen, thank you for your wonderful course and imaginative and thought provoking delivery.

Alison McQuillan
Allez HR Solutions Ltd.

I just wanted to say a huge thank you! I put in my Cosmic Order last Friday after we spoke, and I managed to get two customers on Saturday, but needed just one more. Last night, I was beginning to get worried as it was 8pm and I was still one short. I had to have all three new customers by midnight to qualify. So I went over to a friend's house for a Utility Warehouse 'Girl's-night-in' to have a large glass of wine and to try not to think about it too much!

I was starting to feel gutted that it wasn't going to happen, and guilty that I should be at home making calls rather than drinking wine with team-mates, until I got a text at 10pm from a friend of a friend who asked how she could sign up!!!! My friends were all jumping about with excitement and made me call her there and then and she signed up!! And she turned out to be the perfect customer!

So I just wanted to say thank you for inspiring me to believe, it will change my life. I can't wait until the book launch and I'm sure my friends will be coming too now after seeing the power of Cosmic Ordering!!!

Anna May
Team Leader, Utility Warehouse

You may not realise
it yet,
but you already have,
and already are,
everything
you need.

Ellen has the ability to light up a room with her boundless energy and enthusiasm. A talented trainer, coach, mentor, writer and public speaker; it's rare for one person to have the range of skills which Ellen possesses. And I can honestly say that she 'walks the walk' as much as, if not more than, she 'talks the talk'. I have known Ellen for many years and I have seen her work her magic many, many times.

Ellen's voice makes 'Cosmic Ordering Made Easier' an absolute delight to read. Her beautiful writing style captivates her readers and carries them along on a fun filled journey of enlightenment and encouragement. She provides her reader with both the mindset and the method for success with her clever combination of motivational stories and workbook exercises. Her request to her reader, 'So promise me you'll give yourself the time and do the exercises' illustrates the fact that this book was not written to sit on a bookshelf to collect dust but to be used. I can only compare it to giving someone a golden key which unlocks the door to abundance. However, the door is at the end of a track. The person now has the key and knows where the door is and what's on the other side of it, but to open the door requires an element of faith and a few simple steps. As Ellen tells us, 'Cosmic Ordering is not a passive activity'.

Sali Gray
**Life & Business Coach, Writer, Public Speaker
and Organiser of the Pink Car Rally**